A Travel Guide to the Plains Indian Wars

A TRAVEL GUIDE TO THE PLAINS INDIAN WARS

STAN HOIG

UNIVERSITY OF NEW MEXICO PRESS

Albuquerque

PRINTED IN THE UNITED STATES OF AMERICA

YEAR   PRINTING
12 11 10 09 08 07 06   1 2 3 4 5 6 7

Library of Congress Cataloging-in-Publication Data

Hoig, Stan.
  A travel guide to the Plains Indian wars / Stan Hoig.
      p. cm.
  Includes index.
  ISBN-13: 978-0-8263-3934-8 (pbk. : alk. paper)
  ISBN-10: 0-8263-3934-4 (pbk. : alk. paper)
  1. Indians of North America—Wars—1866–1895—Guidebooks. 2. Indians of North
America—Wars—Great Plains—Guidebooks. 3. Battlefields—Great Plains—
Guidebooks. I. Title.
  E83.866.H65 2006
  978.004'97—dc22

                         2005028715

Book design and composition by Damien Shay
Body type is Utopia 9.5/13
Display is Thunderbird and Edwardian Medium

CONTENTS

ILLUSTRATIONS

MAPS AND DIAGRAMS

PREFACE

Today the deserted remains of Western military posts and the silent sites of battles mark the events of the Plains Indian wars. It is human nature to romanticize this period of American history, but in doing so, we are prone to overlook the great travail endured by both the Native tribes and the soldiers sent to overwhelm them. As a nation, we have finally cast off many of our false notions concerning our nineteenth-century Indian conquest. We can now recognize the rightfulness of Indian resistance and laud the courage of Native peoples in defending their lands even as we appreciate the sacrifice and courage of U.S. soldiers, white and black, who were sent into battle. We understand the simple truth that there were brave men on both sides and why Army officers often lauded the fighting ability and fierce determination of both the Indian warrior and Buffalo Soldier.

The historical remnants of this long war between cultures are fading away and would eventually be gone without the attention of city, state, and federal bodies. Some of our frontier forts have been restored, while some have been totally abandoned, their structures either demolished or sold. Others have been left to rot away or slowly crumble into dust, leaving behind only a half-standing rock chimney or stone wall occasionally inscribed with initials of past occupants—all with a thousand untold events of army life and Indian warfare that were often hard and wearisome, and occasionally filled with moments of great peril.

The concept of frontier forts as compounds surrounded by log stockade walls is seldom accurate. Many did exist, but the natural building materials available in a particular region helped determine the construction and design of a U.S. military fort. When ordered to build a fort in some distant region of the Indian country, army units seldom had time to wait for funds to be appropriated by Congress. Nor were there any manufactured materials present or skilled labor other than what might exist among the troops present to do the building. Fortunately, most men of that day had grown up in rural towns and on farms in America and elsewhere and had had some carpentry and mechanical experience before enlisting in the army.

The choice of a fort location generally depended upon the availability of a water supply for both the men and their animals, timber for fuel, and good pastures for hay and grazing. But streams often ran dry, wood supplies became depleted, and fields were overgrazed. Fort Chadbourne in Texas was abandoned in 1867 when its water supply proved inadequate, and Fort Sill won longevity over Fort Reno in Oklahoma on the argument that the latter's water base was faulty.

Often the military units were forced to live in tents or dugouts until they could construct their own first crude barracks and officer quarters from the green cottonwood, fir, rock, adobe, sod, or other materials at hand. If the fort proved to have a lasting purpose, the Army would eventually upgrade it with buildings constructed of milled lumber or brick. Such materials often had to be wagoned in at great distances, though some forts eventually operated their own sawmills.

The early cottonwood barracks fared badly in the contest with time and weather on the Plains. The logs dried and warped, leaving gaps that wind, dust, and bitter cold invaded in winter. Even those buildings with fireplaces provided little warmth. Bedbugs, fleas, mice, rats, snakes, scorpions, and other intruders were constant annoyances. These in addition to low, leaky roofs, smoky fireplaces, earth or cracked plank floors, and often a lack of glassed windows.

Usually military companies were housed in individual barracks, with their mess halls and kitchens located close by. Food supply was a persistent problem. Frontier posts often selected hunters to procure fresh meat, and it was not uncommon for garrisons to maintain a vegetable garden during the growing season. Disease and poor health often existed among the troops. Some posts were worse than others: Fort Gibson, Indian Territory, once had the reputation among its garrison of being the "Charnel House of the U.S. Army." Although the army tried to maintain at each post a medical person, who was usually designated as an Assistant Surgeon, that person was often poorly trained, overworked, and sorely in need of the few medical supplies that then existed. The archaic method of bleeding as a medical treatment persisted for much of the Indian War years; amputation for those wounded in battle was common.

The nature of quarters on military posts followed the all-important system of rank. Post commanders occupied the best and largest houses while other officers chose their quarters in order of rank and marital status. Married enlisted men, usually noncoms who had been permitted to bring their wives or families to the post, stood next in line. The marriage of an officer or the arrival of a new officer of rank often disrupted the quarters alignment of the entire post, domino fashion.

Normally the barracks, officer quarters, and headquarters buildings were arranged around the post compound with its parade grounds and flag staff. On cavalry posts, as well as others in that day of horse mobility, stables and storehouses were located back away from the compound area. Far in the future, of course, was the day of plumbing, hot water, indoor latrines, refrigeration for maintaining food, cooled air or even electric fans, and other benefits that are known today. Until laundresses could be brought on base, the men took care of their own laundry. But the frontier soldier accepted his privations as the lot of army life. He complained vociferously and continued on.

At the outbreak of the Civil War in 1861, seventy-three military posts existed on the western frontier. The largest number existed in Texas, which had long contested the Comanches and other tribes that resisted the aggressive Anglo-American advance north and westward onto the buffalo prairies. Following the Civil War, westward expansion and increased friction on the Central Plains brought the number of U.S. forts to 116, garrisoned with some 25,000 troops. A shortage of troop strength was a common problem at posts on the frontier, as desertions were far from rare.

The end to most Indian War forts, however, came about as the Indian threat to white settlement diminished in a particular area. Some of the posts—such as Fort Sill; Fort Riley, Kansas; and Fort Robinson, Nebraska—lived on as adjuncts to Indian reservations or were adapted to the techniques of mechanized warfare. A few, like Fort Arbuckle in Oklahoma and the Bozeman Trail forts in Wyoming and Montana, were destroyed during the conflict years by Indian forces.

Time has been kindest to forts in Texas, where weather is drier and winters less severe and native stone was often used in construction. Attention from local and state governments in terms of restoration has also had considerable effect on the preservation of frontier forts. Some, such as Fort Concho and Fort McKavett in Texas and Fort Caspar in Wyoming, stand in excellent restored condition, offering historical support and understanding through their museums and visitor centers. Others like Fort Phantom Hill, Texas, while well worth viewing, thus far lack on-site support. The ruins of Fort Chadbourne are presently being restored by the site's private owner with state help. Fort Phil Kearny, Wyoming, likewise provides a worthy museum and visitor center, though the original structure lacks replication other than a frontal palisade. There are no remaining structures at the site of Fort Dilts, North Dakota. Its remote location and lonely tombstones, however, enhance the story that its markers tell of a corralled wagon train besieged by Indians for two long weeks before a rescue party from Fort Rice finally arrived.

The marking and commemoration of Indian battle sites are also often determined by local authorities and state historical societies, though the federal government has come forth in significant cases. The most notable instance of the latter is the Little Bighorn National Historic Site in Montana. Under the management of the National Park Service, the Little Bighorn site has become the showpiece of the American Indian Wars. Other sites such as the Washita National Battlefield Site in Oklahoma (another Custer-involved site) are federal works in progress.

This guide does not include the fur trade forts of the West, few of which still exist. Because they were generally built from green timber, they failed to stand long under the abrasive weather of their regions. Many of them became convenient fuel for the river boats hauling loads of furs eastward. Only a few, such as Fort Union, North Dakota, still stand in memory of the exciting fur trade period. Some, like Fort Laramie, Wyoming, were purchased for military posts and maintained by the U.S. Army.

The Fetterman Massacre in Wyoming is commemorated by a lone rock monument atop a vantage point that overlooks a forlorn valley landscape where the desperate massacre took place. Roads to some battle locations like that of Killdeer, North Dakota, are inadequately marked and remain somewhat of a challenge to find. But the majority of sites are advantaged by good roads and attractive commemorative markers.

Full appreciation of any fort or battle site, however, requires a knowledge of its history. General information is normally provided on the site's historical plaque. Visitors can learn far more about the event through the fare of on-site museums and visitor centers that offer well-studied books and personal accounts, archival records, exhibits, brochures, lectures, and personal guides.

Such professional help greatly increases the pleasure and vicarious adventure of any visit to a historic site. I personally wish to thank those persons at various sites who graciously provided information that aided me in preparing this tour guide.

Stan Hoig

PART ONE

The Plains Indian Wars

CHAPTER ONE

Beyond Missouri: Discovering the Wondrous West

Today's roadway tourists can find bountiful historical lore of America's Indian Wars of the Great Plains. To the south are the frontier forts of Texas, some handsomely restored and some standing as ghostly remnants of a day gone by. They evoke images of blue-coated cavalry troops riding forth to scour the arid vistas of the Llano Estacado. While standing on a deserted army parade ground, you will need little imagination to hear the sharp notes of a bugle sounding reveille at morning call or the resonant tones of taps to end the day.

A visit to the short-grassed prairies of the Texas Panhandle and western Oklahoma lets one vicariously ride the trails of Custer, Mackenzie, and Miles leading to the Washita, Palo Duro Canyon, and other celebrated battle sites. And who can view the time-sculptured buttes of Wyoming and Montana without envisioning atop them the determined warriors of Red Cloud, Crazy Horse, or Sitting Bull?

The classic Indian battle of them all—the Sioux/Northern Cheyenne victory over Custer and his Seventh Cavalry on the bloody ridge overlooking the Little Bighorn—is dramatically recounted at the Little Bighorn Battlefield National Historic Site of Montana. And at Wounded Knee in South Dakota, the tragic finale of the Indian wars was written in blood.

Add to these Washita, Palo Duro Canyon, Beecher's Island, Punished Woman's Fork, Adobe Walls, Platte Bridge, Fetterman Massacre, Sand

Creek Massacre, Hayfield, Wagon Box, Corn Train Massacre, Bluewater, Howard Wells, Soldier Springs, Fort Robinson, Whitestone Hill, Sappa Creek, Pawnee Fork.

Buffalo Wallow, Lyman Wagon Train, Plum Creek, Little Robe Creek, Hennessey Massacre, Turkey Springs, Wichita Agency, Wichita Village, Chouteau's Island, Kidder Massacre, Lone Tree Massacre, Crooked Creek, Julesburg, Summit Springs, Bear Paw, Big Hole, Canyon Creek, Rosebud, Lame Deer, Powder River, Wolf Mountain, Arikara Village, Slim Buttes, and hundreds of other engagements tell the sad and bloody story.

But there is more to Plains history than warfare. Embedded in its memory are phantasmal images of wandering dinosaurs and other prehistoric creatures, long tribal migrations across the prairie, Spanish conquistadors searching for gold, exploring parties seeking out the region's mysteries, trappers and hunters combing the virgin streams, steamboats plying the Muddy Missouri and other navigable streams, railroad gangs stretching their iron rails across the land, cowboys pushing bellowing cattle herds north from Texas, and a host of legendary figures such as Bridger, Carson, Custer, and Sitting Bull whose names haunt our Western past.

A journey along the route of the Santa Fe Trail in Kansas invites images of ox-train caravans lumbering toward Santa Fe. Similarly, the Platte River Trail through Kansas, Nebraska, and Wyoming retraces a road once flooded by the Conestoga wagons of immigrants headed for Oregon, Utah, and other regions of the Far West. These famous routes lead the tourist, even as they did the early pioneers, westward toward the bright, beckoning peaks of the Rocky Mountains.

The cross poles of Indian tepees no longer dress the river banks; the great herds of buffalo that once blackened the valleys are gone; highways and fences divide the land; and cities loom ever more threateningly. Still, a visitor to the Plains will be witnessing the same broad prairies, slashed by serpentine channels and studded with timeless plateaus. A sense of openness and serenity prevails, and it is possible to understand not only the spiritual devotion of its native people to their Mother Earth but the awesome adventure known to those who came exploring.

After 1800, U.S.-sponsored expeditions opened windows of worldview to the Great Plains and its Indian tribes. These exciting and colorful pageants of discovery predestined critical contests of proprietorship between Indians and advancing whites. For the Native American there was the travail of white intrusion and eventual subjugation. For

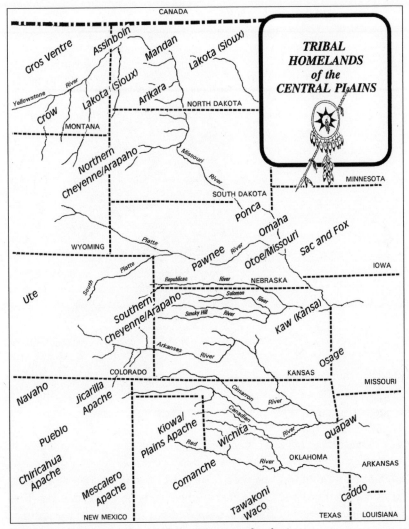

Tribal homelands of the Central Plains. (Courtesy of author)

non-Indian Americans, civilian and soldier alike, dire dangers thrived upon the far-flung prairies where heat and dust and thirst and the wear of pathless travel were ever present. Remembrance of this enhances our empathy with the past as we gaze upon the ruins of frontier forts, read historical markers, tour battle sites, or learn from studied histories and the fare of museums.

Meriwether Lewis.
(*Appleton's Cyclopedia of
American Biography*)

Thomas Jefferson's purchase of the Louisiana Territory in 1804
ignited a great interest in the vast lands that the newly created United
States claimed west of the Mississippi River. In an effort to establish
U.S. autonomy over the region and to discover its resource potential,
Jefferson sent Meriwether Lewis and William Clark up the Missouri
River to the Pacific in 1804. Principally an exploration and scientific
adventure, the Lewis and Clark Expedition initiated the first U.S. rela-
tions with native peoples on the Great Plains.

The explorers constructed a winter camp called Fort Mandan
near present Bismarck, North Dakota, before pushing on across the
Rocky Mountains to the Pacific Coast. When they returned to St. Louis
in September 1806, they brought dried plants, rock specimens, and

William Clark.
(*Appleton's Cyclopedia of American Biography*)

artifacts of Western Indian life. It was an introduction to the wondrous West beyond the Mississippi River for many Americans. But the Lewis and Clark Expedition also marked the beginning of a long and troubled relationship between the American nation and the native occupants of that new world.

Spain and the United States were still contesting the boundaries of the Louisiana Purchase when Capt. Zebulon M. Pike set out in 1806 with his twenty-five "Dam'd set of rascels" to explore the upper Arkansas and Red Rivers. There he hoped to contact the Osages, Pawnees, Comanches, and other tribes of the region and win their allegiance to the United States. After visiting the Osages in southwest Missouri, Pike pushed on to a Pawnee village on the Republican River in present Nebraska. Though the party was received well, the Pawnees insisted that Pike not continue on into the country of their enemies. In

Zebulon Pike.
(*Appleton's Cyclopedia of American Biography*)

doing so, Pike was forced to defy some five hundred warriors who surrounded the group with strung bows, spears, and tomahawks. Marching south to the Great Bend of the Arkansas River, he dispatched a small party under Lt. James B. Wilkinson to explore southeastward down the stream to Arkansas. Pike, meanwhile, continued on into the Rocky Mountains of Colorado, where he was captured by Spanish forces of New Mexico province and held as a spy. He was eventually released and permitted to return to the States.

Civilian entrepreneurs, as well, explored the West. Fur trader Manuel Lisa led a fur-garnering expedition up the Missouri River in 1807. At the mouth of the Platte he met adventurer John Colter, who had already made two trips up the river. Colter joined the fur traders and was with Lisa when he established Fort Manuel at the mouth of the Yellowstone. From there Colter was sent out to bring Indians in to trade, and in doing so became the first white man to witness the wonders of today's Yellowstone National Park.

Two penetrations of the Plains occurred in 1811. During that spring George Sibley, a factor at Fort Osage, Missouri, accompanied a party of Osage Indians through Kansas to the Salt Plains of the Cimarron River in present northwest Oklahoma. At the same time the Astorians under Wilson Price Hunt moved up the Missouri River from St. Louis in keelboats on their difficult voyage to establish a settlement in the Pacific Northwest. While returning east from Fort Astoria on the Columbia River in 1812, Robert Stuart and six other men discovered the important South Pass of present Wyoming.

It was 1820 before the United States sent another scientific exploration into the West, this one under Maj. Stephen Long. He and his nineteen men moved by horseback into central Nebraska. There on the Loup River, Long conducted peace talks with the Pawnees before marching on up the Platte and South Platte into present Colorado. After examining the animal and plant life of the region and ascending Pike's Peak, the party divided on the Arkansas River. One segment under Capt. John R. Bell continued on downriver to Fort Smith, Arkansas, while the remainder under Long rode south and, mistaking the Canadian River for the Red River, followed it eastward across present Oklahoma.

In 1822 William Ashley's band of fur trappers plied the headwaters of the Green and Platte Rivers of Wyoming. Thomas Fitzpatrick, Jedediah Smith, William Jackson, William Sublette, Robert Campbell, and a host of other mountain men soon followed. Behind these came missionaries Samuel Parker, Marcus Whitman, and Father Pierre de Smet leading settlers to the Oregon country.

Initially the principal interest of the U.S. Government was focused on the fur-rich mountains and the fertile lands of California and Oregon. The Plains were still considered to be largely desert inhabited by unruly bands. Soon the region between the Mississippi and the Rocky Mountains came to be looked upon as a place to which the unwanted tribes of the East and South could be removed away from the ever-pressing white advance. In 1825 Congress officially designated areas in present North and South Dakota, Nebraska, Kansas, and Oklahoma for that purpose under the title of "Indian Territory." The reserved areas in Nebraska and Kansas would eventually fall to the pressures of white settlement, leaving Indian Territory to comprise most of present Oklahoma.

That same year, the Atkinson-O'Fallon expedition set sail up the Missouri River to consummate treaties with the tribes along that waterway. Its aim was to provide protection for the lucrative fur trade. Under the command of Gen. Henry Atkinson, the expedition departed St. Louis during early March in nine keelboats propelled by manually operated paddle wheels, sails, oars, and cordelles. Moving slowly upriver, the commissioners initiated agreements with the Ponca, Arikara, Mandan, Crow, Missouri, Pawnee, Omaha, Sioux, and Cheyenne Indians. By these pacts, it was promised that the United States would hold trade with the tribes and receive them under its protection.

On July 4, the commissioners met with the Oglalas and Cheyennes at the mouth of the Teton River, presently the site of Pierre, South Dakota. Typically, the Indians were gracious hosts. The commissioners and military officers were invited to a feast at the Oglala camp. An arrangement of beaver skins and pieces of colorful cloth dressed the center of a large lodge. A ceremonial calumet lay charged and ready across a row of buffalo dung. After the pipe had been passed about, the commissioners were treated to a meal of thirteen dogs boiled in kettles and drinking water that had been brought up from the Missouri River in buffalo paunches. In an exchange of gifts, Cheyenne chief High-backed Wolf presented the general with a fine-looking mule equipped with Spanish accouterments. The troops fired artillery across the river, the exploding shells greatly impressing the tribesmen.

Continuing on upriver, the expedition conducted treaties of peaceful intent and trade with the Arikaras, Mandans, Gros Ventres, and Crows. Camp Barbour was established at the mouth of the Yellowstone River, the party there meeting William Ashley and his mountain men who arrived bearing a hundred packs of beaver pelts.

During the decade of the 1820s, commerce began on the Santa Fe Trail, opening trade between Missouri and New Mexico. Already fur trappers and hunters were trekking from St. Louis up the Missouri and other easterly flowing streams to the Rocky Mountains, making contact with the tribes of the Great Plains and introducing the goods of the white man's world to them.

While on their way to the annual trappers' rendezvous in 1834, William Sublette and Robert Campbell constructed a log stockade called Fort William where the Laramie River joins the Platte. Eventually it became known as Fort Laramie. Soon this was followed by other trading posts such as Bent's Fort on the Arkansas River of present

Colorado, St. Vrain's on the South Platte, Jim Bridger's post in far southwestern Wyoming, and Fort Union on the upper Missouri.

In 1835, Col. Henry Dodge led an exploring expedition of some 125 men to the Rocky Mountains of Colorado. The party marched up the Platte and South Platte Rivers and then south past the site of present Denver to Pueblo, where the firm of Gantt and Blackwell operated a trading post. Turning eastward along the Arkansas River, Dodge's party met a formidable-looking but friendly Cheyenne war party armed with war shields, spears, bows, and arrows. Their village was encamped along the river near another fort operated by the Bent brothers and Ceran St. Vrain. There the expedition witnessed the effects of white influence on the natives who, having been supplied with a keg of whiskey by unscrupulous traders, were involved in a drunken orgy.

Such instances were seen as omens to many Indian leaders. Soon they would realize that white intrusion onto their lands threatened not only the buffalo and other game upon which they critically depended but their very identity as a people. A long, bitter war for control of the Great Plains would soon begin. Accounts of this great clash of cultures abound in our literature, but much of it also lies etched in battle sites, abandoned posts, and forgotten graves across the American West.

Books to Read

Ambrose, Stephen E. *Undaunted Courage.* New York: Simon & Schuster, 1996.

Farnham, Thomas J. *Travels in the Great Western Prairies, the Anahuac and Rocky Mountains, and in Oregon Territory.* New York: Greeley & McElrath, 1843.

Gregg, Josiah. *Commerce of the Prairies.* Ed. by Max L. Moorhead. Norman: University of Oklahoma Press, 1954.

Hoig, Stan. *Beyond the Frontier: Exploring the Indian Country.* Norman: University of Oklahoma Press, 1998.

Horgan, Paul. *Josiah Gregg and His Vision of the Early West.* New York: Farrar Straus Giroux, 1941.

Inman, Col. Henry. *The Old Santa Fe Trail.* New York: The Macmillan Company, 1897.

Irving, Washington. *A Tour of the Prairies.* Ed. by John Francis McDermott. Norman: University of Oklahoma Press, 1956.

Jackson, Donald, ed. and annot. *The Journals of Zebulon Montgomery Pike, with Letters and Related Documents.* 2 vols. Norman: University of Oklahoma Press, 1966.

James, Edwin. *An Account of an Expedition from Pittsburgh to the Rocky Mountains.* 2 vols. Ann Arbor, Mich.: University Microfilms, 1966.

John, Elizabeth A. *Storms Brewed in Other Men's Worlds.* College Station: Texas A&M University Press, 1975.

Morgan, Dale L. *Jedediah Smith and the Opening of the West.* Lincoln: University of Nebraska, 1972.

CHAPTER TWO

Comanche Challenge: Wars of the Southern Plains

Countless engagements mark the course of Texas history. *The Old Army in Texas*, by Thomas T. Smith, lists over two hundred combat actions against the Indians by the U.S. Army in Texas between 1849 and 1881, this number not including Spanish, Texas Ranger, and Texas militia actions. Many of the Texas conflict sites have become obscured to record, but some of the more notable clashes can be identified. The Norteño massacre of the Franciscan mission on the San Saba River is recalled by its ruins and those of its attendant presidio at Menard, Texas. In March 1758, a swarm of Comanches and their allies appeared on the San Saba with their faces painted black and crimson for war, the tails of wild animals hanging down about their heads. After confiscating horses and food, the attackers killed two of the mission's priests and mutilated their bodies before sacking the buildings and setting the church on fire. Soldiers at the nearby presidio under Don Diego Ortiz Parrilla remained inside its walls to protect the 237 women and children who had taken refuge there.

In an effort to halt the Norteño attacks, Parrilla organized an army of nearly five hundred presidio soldiers, mounted militia, and Indian allies the following year. He led his command northward to where the Taovayas held forth in two villages that straddled the Red River near present Spanish Fort, Texas. A Comanche village was camped nearby. Parrilla's army was met with a swooping attack by a well-prepared warrior force

Sam Houston.
(*Appleton's Cyclopedia of
American Biography*)

armed with French muskets. The ferocity of the Taovayas, their strength
of some six thousand warriors, and the fortification of their village dismayed the Spaniards and their Indian allies. They turned about and
retreated in such chaos that Parrilla's two brass cannons were abandoned. Eleven soldiers and two of the Indian allies were killed in the
fight. The defeat was so demoralizing as to discourage further aggressive
ventures by the Spaniards.

James Bowie and his brother Razin were involved in a battle that
was fought near the San Saba mission in 1831. The two were among a
party of twelve men who were searching for a lost Spanish silver mine
when they came under attack by a large group of Tawakoni and Waco
warriors. The men managed to hold off their attackers for eight days
with only one of their group being killed. When the Indians finally

retired, the Bowies and their comrades made their way back to the safety of San Antonio.

A noteworthy event that occurred in 1836, the year of independence for the Republic of Texas, is memorialized by Parker's Fort, the initial settlement of Limestone County on the Navasota River near present Groesbeck. There Comanche and Kiowa raiders captured nine-year-old Cynthia Ann Parker, who married into the tribe and ultimately became mother to the famous Comanche chief Quanah Parker.

The foundling Republic of Texas under Sam Houston attempted to pacify tribes in its north and west that vigorously opposed the white settlement steadily pushing out from the coastal region beyond San Antonio and the Austin settlement. In February 1838, a large party of Comanche warriors appeared at San Antonio to request that the Texans meet and talk peace with their chiefs some 250 miles north. The Texans did so, but they and the Comanches could not agree on a line of separation. More talks were held later that spring, but the same disagreements prevailed.

Upon replacing the Indian-sympathizing Houston as president of the Republic, however, Mirabeau B. Lamar initiated an aggressive policy of punitive action against the tribes. In early 1839, a force of Texas Rangers, aided by Lipan Apache and Anadarko scouts, marched to the San Saba River and launched an early morning attack on a Comanche camp, killing forty-six of the villagers. Later that spring, the Comanches retaliated when some 240 of their warriors ambushed and killed seven Texas Rangers north of Austin.

During this same year, the Lamar administration took action to expel a large body of Cherokee Indians who had migrated from the Arkansas River into East Texas. Lamar directed forces under Gen. Thomas Rusk to remove the Cherokees from Texas soil. On July 15, 1839, Rusk attacked them on the Neches River, killing Chief John Bowle, a close friend of Sam Houston, and drove them across the Red River into southeastern Indian Territory.

A bloody massacre ensued the following year when chiefs of the Comanches, the largest and most dominant tribe, were invited to San Antonio for a peace conference. Though they arrived at the Texas settlement under a flag of truce, the wary Comanches refused to surrender their bows, arrows, and knives upon being ushered into the small courthouse for talks. As a peace offering they had brought along a white captive, sixteen-year-old Matilda Lockhart. Infuriated by her abused appearance, the Texas leaders attempted to take the Comanche chiefs

A Comanche warrior. (Thrall, *Pictorial History of Texas*)

hostage against the release of other white captives. The Comanches sounded their war cry and fought back. Many of them fell under a barrage of gunfire. When the smoke had cleared, some thirty-three Comanches, including women and children along with several leading chiefs, lay dead. A captured woman was placed on a horse and sent to tell her people that if the other captives were not released in twelve

When Texas was a Mexican Province, the Comanches often traded in San Antonio. (Western History Collection, University of Oklahoma)

days, the remaining Comanches at San Antonio would be executed. Instead of releasing their captives, the enraged Indians tortured many of them to death.

The Comanches further responded with a massive invasion of settlements along the Texas Gulf Coast. Under war leader Buffalo Hump, a huge war party was organized on the Edwards Plateau. Bypassing the fortified San Antonio, the Comanches struck the undefended towns of Victoria and Linnville, killing citizens and ravaging the countryside. The jubilant warriors, loaded with spoils of their raid, were returning north when they were intercepted at Plum Creek north of San Antonio by a makeshift force of Texas Rangers and Tonkawa allies under Capt. Ben McCulloch. Badly mauled, Buffalo Hump's raiders left over eighty dead on the field before escaping the Texas onslaught.

Following this action, Col. John Moore of the Texas Rangers, accompanied by Lipan Apache scouts, conducted a series of Indian-hunting forays into the tribal lands of western Texas. On one occasion, they located a Comanche village on the Colorado River west of present Abilene, Texas, and attacked it. By Moore's estimate, forty-eight tribespeople were left dead on the ground and some eighty more were either killed or drowned while attempting to flee across the river.

In 1841, Capt. Jack Hays and thirty-five Texas Rangers killed ten Comanches and captured two others west of San Antonio. Later on the Llano River, he attacked a Comanche village on the move, killing several of its members in a running fight.

Upon returning to the Texas presidency in 1841, Sam Houston set out to make peace with the Comanches and other tribes. When the Comanches refused to attend a peace council at Bird's Fort just north of present Fort Worth, Houston sent peace emissary Joseph C. Eldridge across the Red River into southwestern Indian Territory. Eldridge, however, failed to persuade Comanche chief Pahhauca to attend a peace council at Bird's Fort in September 1843. Pahhauca was also absent from a peace council conducted the following November on the Red River opposite the mouth of Cache Creek by Cherokee agent Pierce M. Butler. Through the efforts of Cherokee frontiersman Jesse Chisholm, the Comanches were persuaded to attend a Texas-sponsored event at Council Springs near present Waco, Texas, in the fall of 1844. Sam Houston himself rode up from the Texas capital at Washington-on-the-Brazos to attend the meeting.

"Six years ago I made peace with the Comanches," he told the circle of chiefs. "That peace was kept until a bad chief took my place. That chief made war on the Comanches and murdered them at San Antonio. He made war on the Cherokees, also, and drove them from the country. Now this has to be mended; war can do us no good."[1]

Houston suggested that a dividing line between the Comanches and Texas be established, to run south from the Red River below the Wichita Mountains to the old mission on the San Saba River and from there to the Rio Grande. Texas, he said, would establish a series of forts along that line. The Comanches refused to agree to this, but they did sign a less binding friendship pact.

Following the annexation of Texas as a state of the Union in 1846, the United States sponsored another major conference at the Council Springs site. A pact known as the Treaty of Comanche Peak (Comanche Peak near Fort Worth being the site scheduled before the council was moved) was signed, and a delegation of Indian leaders was escorted to Washington, DC. This effort likewise failed to end the warfare.

Still another peace effort was made in late 1850 when Texas special agent John H. Rollins, accompanied by Indian agents Robert Neighbors and John S. Ford, interpreter Jesse Chisholm, and Delaware tribal leader John Connor, met with the Comanches under Buffalo Hump and other

After the battle, a surprising fact was discovered. Stripping the robe from the fallen medicine man, Pohebits-Quasho, the Rangers discovered that he wore a coat of Spanish mail that had somehow survived among the Indians from the time of the Conquistadors' visit to the Plains.

The success of the Ford strike into Indian Territory opened the door for similar intrusion by the commander of the U.S. Texas Military District, Lt. Gen. David Twiggs. Twiggs sent a battalion of Second U.S. Cavalry under Maj. Earl Van Dorn to establish a military camp on Otter Creek just north of the Red River. It was named Camp Radziminski in honor of a Polish-born officer who had died a short time before.

In September 1858, Van Dorn launched an attack on a party of Comanches that was camped at a Wichita village east of the Wichita Mountains. The Comanches, under Chief Buffalo Hump, were on their way to conduct peace talks with U.S. officials at Fort Arbuckle. Making an all-night march around the Wichita Mountains with four troops of Second Cavalry, Van Dorn fell on the unsuspecting peace caravan. When it was over, seventy Indians lay dead on the field. Van Dorn's men ravaged the encampment, burning 120 lodges to the ground and capturing most of the Comanches' invaluable horse herd. In addition, the peaceful Wichitas, the first known occupants of the region, suffered many losses of their own. Five of Van Dorn's men were killed. Among the dead was West Pointer Lt. Cornelius Van Camp who took an arrow in the heart.

Van Dorn levied still another strike upon the Comanches during the spring of 1859. In hopes of removing his people from harm's way, Buffalo Hump had moved his band north into southern Kansas. Still Van Dorn found them. Marching up from Camp Radziminski, on May 13 Van Dorn's scouts discovered the Comanche camp on Crooked Creek in present Meade County, Kansas. Once again, the tribe suffered badly, with forty-nine dead and thirty-seven captured.

The domain of the native tribes south of the Arkansas River also became threatened by the advance of United States interests and the relocation of emigrant tribes into the Indian Territory. By the mid-1830s, the five principal tribes of the South—the Cherokee, Creek, Choctaw, Chickasaw, and Seminole—along with others from the East had been relocated in eastern Indian Territory. The Cross Timbers, a growth of scrub oak and blackjack that stretched southward across the center of the territory and well into Texas, provided a natural division between the more domesticated newcomers and the wilder Plains tribes.

Conflicts between the two groups, however, quickly developed. The Plains Indians were angered by the intrusion of hunting parties from the emigrant tribes, while the latter suffered from raids on their livestock by war parties from the west. In an effort to resolve these conflicts and to monitor the emigrant tribes in their new locations, the United States established Fort Gibson on the Neosho River of Indian Territory and Fort Towson on the Red River.

In 1834, following the kidnapping of a dragoon officer by unknown Indians and the murder of Judge Gabriel Martin, a white planter who resided along the Red River, plus the kidnapping of Martin's nine-year-old son and a slave, the United States moved to contact the tribes in western Indian Territory. Gen. Henry Leavenworth commanded the large military expedition that marched from Fort Gibson in July. En route, a strange malady struck both the men and animals of the expedition. Near the mouth of the Washita, Leavenworth himself became deathly ill and turned command of the decimated dragoon regiment over to Col. Henry Dodge. Leavenworth died soon after.

Pushing on west to the Wichita Mountains, Dodge encountered a large, friendly Comanche village and camped nearby. The Comanches directed him farther west to a Wichita village on the North Fork of the Red River. There Dodge was able to rescue young Martin and his father's slave. Dodge also made a first official contact with a band of Kiowas who arrived at the village. He persuaded a delegation of Comanches, Wichitas, and Kiowas to accompany him back to Fort Gibson to arrange preliminary peace talks. A full peace council was held during the summer of 1835 at newly established Camp Mason near present Norman, Oklahoma. The treaty talks, which suffered from hot, dry weather and late arrival of the peace commissioners, were largely unsuccessful. The United States, however, established Fort Holmes near the site, and Col. A. P. Chouteau conducted trade there until his death in 1838.

To give further protection to the emigrant tribes, the United States constructed Fort Washita in 1842 near the Leavenworth expedition's former campsite on the Washita River. With the advent of the California Gold Rush of 1849–50 and the opening of a westward route along the Canadian River, the United States directed military explorer Capt. Randolph B. Marcy to establish Fort Arbuckle south of the Washita River during the spring of 1851. The fort would oversee the Indians of the region until the beginning of the Civil War.

During the fall of 1859, the federal government supported the wish of Texas to purge itself entirely of Indian tribes. The Brazos reserve Indians were removed from Texas and marched to a reservation area in western Indian Territory that had been leased from the Choctaw and Chickasaw Nations. The once-powerful Comanches along with the Caddos, Anadarkos, Tawakonis, Wacos, Ionis, and Wichitas were placed under the jurisdiction of a newly created Wichita Indian agency on the Washita River. Fort Cobb, a small post of stockade shacks, was erected close by to provide military oversight for the agency.

At the outbreak of the Civil War, Union forces were withdrawn. Fort Cobb was occupied by Texas Confederate forces briefly, while former Union agent Matthew Leeper assumed responsibility for the Indians for the Confederacy. Rebel general Albert Pike arrived at the agency on August 6, 1861, to initiate treaties with the Plains tribes of the region. On the night of October 23, 1862, Union-sympathizing Indians from Kansas massacred and torched the agency, murdering many of the Texas-aligned Tonkawas who were camped nearby. Realizing that the Rebel forces could provide them little protection or subsistence, many of the smaller tribes of the agency fled to Kansas, where they settled near trader Jesse Chisholm, who had also moved north to the mouth of the Little Arkansas.

Texas had rid itself of most of its native tribal population. But the former Republic would find that Indian raiding of its frontier settlements had by no means ended.

Books to Read

Bolton, Herbert E. *Athanase de Méziéres and the Louisiana-Texas Frontier, 1768–1780*. 2 vols. Cleveland: Arthur H. Clark Co., 1914.

Chalfant, William Y. *Without Quarter: The Wichita Expedition and the Fight on Crooked Creek*. Norman: University of Oklahoma Press, 1991.

DeShields, James T. *Border Wars of Texas*. Tioga, TX: The Herald Company, 1912.

Frazer, Robert W. *Forts of the West*. Norman: University of Oklahoma Press, 1965, 1972.

Hoig, Stan. *Tribal Wars of the Southern Plains*. Norman: University of Oklahoma Press, 1993.

Richardson, Rupert Norval. *The Comanche Barrier to South Plains Settlement*. Glendale, CA: Arthur H. Clark Co., 1933.

———. *The Frontier of Northwest Texas, 1846 to 1876*. Glendale: Arthur H. Clark Co., 1963.

Salvant, J. U., and Robert M. Utley. *Historic Forts of Texas*. Austin: University Press of Texas, 1991.

Smith, Thomas T. *The Old Army in Texas: A Research Guide to the U.S. Army in Nineteenth-Century Texas*. Austin: Texas State Historical Association, 2000.

Wallace, Ernest, and E. Adamson Hoebel. *The Comanches, Lords of the South Plains*. Norman: University of Oklahoma Press, 1952.

Wilbarger, J. W. *Indian Depredations in Texas*. Austin: Hutchings Printing House, 1889.

Note

1. Jonnie Wallis, *Sixty Years on the Brazos: The Life and Letters of John Washington Lockhart* (Los Angeles: Private printing, 1930), 98.

William S. Harney.
(*Leslie's Illustrated
Newspaper*)

Sioux at Fort Laramie left three Indians dead and several wounded. During August 1854, a fracas that ignited over the shooting of a stray Mormon cow by a Sioux was exacerbated when arrogant, Indian-hating Lt. John Grattan invaded the Sioux village with twenty-nine men, an interpreter, and two artillery pieces. When he attempted to make an arrest, the tribesmen resisted and shooting began. Grattan and all of his men but one were slain. That one, who had his tongue cut out, died later at Fort Laramie.

Sporadic friction continued along the Platte Trail until U.S. officials concluded that the Indians must be punished. In the fall of 1855, Gen. William S. Harney marched from Fort Leavenworth with six hundred men to Ash Hollow, west of present Ogallala, Nebraska. There he found an encampment of Brule Sioux Indians under Chief Little Thunder. Ignoring Little Thunder's declaration of friendship, Harney ordered his troops to attack the village from two sides. Eighty-six Indians were killed, and a like number of women and children were taken prisoner.

E. V. Sumner.
(*Appleton's Cyclopedia of
American Biography*)

Still another major effort to chastise the Indians of the Central
Plains took place in 1857. An army unit under the command of Col. E. V.
Sumner outfitted at Fort Leavenworth for a campaign against the
Cheyennes. Sumner divided his forces into two columns. One, led by
himself, marched up the Platte River past newly established Forts
Kearny and Grattan to Fort Laramie, where he turned south along the
Rocky Mountains. Another column, under the command of Maj. John
Sedgwick, headed down the Santa Fe Trail that struck and followed the
Arkansas River past Fort Atkinson to Bent's Fort and Pueblo. There he
swung north along the Rockies. The objective was for the two columns
to make a juncture on the South Platte near the ruins of the vacated
Fort St. Vrain.

This they did on July 5. Informed by his Pawnee scouts that the
Cheyennes were camped on Beaver Creek in northwestern Kansas,
Sumner reorganized his troops and began a southeastward march on
the thirteenth. The Cheyennes had moved to the Solomon River where

John Sedgwick.
(*Appleton's Cyclopedia of American Biography*)

Sumner found and attacked them on July 29. The Cheyennes had made their battle medicine. Painted and decked in their war bonnets, they waited in line as Sumner's cavalry, three hundred strong, approached. The warriors were supported in the belief that, as their medicine men had told them, the soldiers' bullets would fall harmlessly to the ground before them.

But when Sumner surprisingly ordered his men to "draw sabres," the sight of the long blades flashing in the sun shocked and demoralized the warriors. Firing a shower of arrows that had little effect, the Cheyennes fled in disarray, breaking into small parties as the troops pursued. In the isolated fights that took place, two troopers were killed and nine wounded, among the latter being Lt. J. E. B. Stuart, who would later become famous as the head of cavalry for the Confederacy. There was no precise accounting of how many casualties the Cheyennes had suffered, though Sumner estimated that nine warriors had been killed and a good many wounded.

Bent's Fort on the Arkansas River. (Inman, *The Old Santa Fe Trail*)

Even as the Northern and Southern states moved inexorably toward their great national conflict, a series of Indian engagements were being fought across the Central Plains from the Dakotas to Texas. A major area of turmoil was that of Colorado Territory where clashes between whites and Indians along the Oregon and Santa Fe Trails increased drastically due to the discovery of gold on Cherry Creek and the resulting flood of gold seekers during 1858 and 1859.

The beleaguered army attempted to protect the Western trails. Stuart, still active in the region, pursued raiders in the vicinity of Bent's Fort, capturing the wife and family of Kiowa chief Satank. At the same time, Capt. Samuel D. Sturgis led a force of dragoons from Fort Cobb, Indian Territory, north to the Republican River, where he engaged some six hundred Kiowas and Comanches in battle. But when the already undermanned army was further decimated by resignations of officers going over to the South, the tribes on the Plains were left free to raid pretty much at will.

By the Treaty of Fort Laramie, the United States had defined the homeland of the Cheyennes and Arapahos as lying between the Platte and Arkansas Rivers from western Kansas to the main range of the Rocky Mountains, the major portion thus being Colorado Territory. The government retained only the rights of establishing roads and military posts therein. With the gold rush, however, came white occupancy in the form of permanent settlements, a principal one being foundling Denver City at the mouth of Cherry Creek.

J. E. B. Stuart.
(*Appleton's Cyclopedia of American Biography*)

In an effort to establish U.S. claim to the territory, Commissioner of Indian Affairs A. B. Greenwood met with Cheyenne and Arapaho chiefs at Fort Wise (soon to be renamed Fort Lyon) on the Arkansas River just downriver from Bent's Fort. By a treaty initiated there in 1860, the chiefs were persuaded to give up claim to the lands assigned to them at Fort Laramie and agree to settle on a small, gameless reservation in eastern Colorado Territory. The tribes soon realized their error and recanted the treaty.

White citizens in Colorado viewed the region not as a legally established Indian homeland but as an extension of American empire. Though the tribes offered little if any resistance to the massive intrusion of their lands, clashes, largely white initiated, soon erupted. The 1862 Sioux massacre of whites in Minnesota further ignited fears among Colorado settlers that the Cheyennes and Arapahos were preparing to conduct a similar "war of extermination." These fears were exploited for political reasons by Territorial Governor John Evans and Col. John M. Chivington, who commanded the U.S. military in Colorado.

John M. Chivington.
(*Leslie's Illustrated
Newspaper*)

During the spring of 1864 following reports of stolen stock, Chivington sent his First Colorado Cavalry troops against the Indians. Troops under Lt. Clark Dunn and Maj. Jacob Downing attacked Cheyenne camps along the South Platte trail north of Denver. A number of Cheyennes were killed. At the same time, Lt. George S. Eayre led a fifty-four-man unit on a foray to Beaver Creek east of Denver, torching two recently evacuated villages and capturing their supplies and equipage.

Returning to Denver, Eayre reoutfitted and marched eastward well into Kansas. On the Smoky Hill River some forty miles north of Fort Larned, Kansas, he came onto a Cheyenne buffalo hunt. The hunt was headed by Cheyenne chief Lean Bear, who the year before had attended a peace conference at Washington, DC. There Lean Bear had talked with President Abraham Lincoln, asking protection from U.S. troops on the Plains. Lincoln had explained sympathetically that as a father could not always control his children, he could not always control his troops.

Persons of note in this 1864 Denver photo include (back row) the blonde-headed Jack Smith and John S. Smith. On the far left (seated) is Cheyenne chief White Antelope, Arapaho chief Neva, Black Kettle, and to his left Dog Soldier leader Bull Bear. Maj. Edward Wynkoop (with cigar) and Capt. Silas Soule kneel in front. (Courtesy of Colorado Historical Society Library)

Upon seeing Eayre's troops, Lean Bear and another chief named Star rode to meet them to show a paper that vouched for their peacefulness. In doing so, however, both Cheyenne leaders were shot from their saddles without warning and killed. A running battle ensued with Eayre having four of his men killed and three wounded. The Cheyennes drove the troops from the field and to refuge at Fort Larned. The unwarranted murder of their two chiefs infuriated the Cheyenne Dog Soldiers. Led by Bull Bear, brother to Lean Bear, the Dog Soldiers vented their wrath upon settlements in Kansas and transportation along the two migration trails.

In an attempt to end the fighting, Cheyenne principal chief Black Kettle responded to a plea from trader William Bent for peace. He sent a message by elderly subchief One-Eye to Fort Lyon, where Maj. Edward Wynkoop was in command, proposing an exchange of prisoners and an end to the fighting. Wynkoop was impressed with One-Eye's bravery and accepted the offer, leading an expedition of some 120 to 130 First Colorado Cavalry to the Smoky Hill River to meet with the Cheyennes.

There he persuaded Black Kettle and seven other Cheyenne and Arapaho chiefs to accompany him to Camp Weld at Denver for peace talks with Governor Evans.

During the Camp Weld council, the Indians conferred with Evans and Chivington. In the end, Chivington told Black Kettle and the chiefs to take their people to Fort Lyon and submit to military authority. Though Chivington did not specifically say so, he strongly implied that if the Indians went to Lyon, they would be safe from attack. "You are nearer to Major Wynkoop than any one else," he instructed them, "and you can go to him when you get ready to do that."[2]

Even as Black Kettle's group was en route to Denver to talk peace, matters on the Santa Fe Trail had heated up. The Kiowas under Satanta attacked a wagon train near Cimarron Springs at the very southwestern tip of Kansas, killing ten teamsters and running off the stock. Still another train had been attacked some sixty miles above Fort Larned, near where Fort Dodge would be located the following year. Maj. Gen. James Blunt, commanding the District of the Upper Arkansas, concluded that the "red devils needed a little killing" and launched a punitive expedition from Fort Riley.

Marching to Fort Larned, where he was joined by Maj. Scott J. Anthony and two companies of First Colorado Cavalry, Blunt led his four-hundred-man army up the Santa Fe Trail to Cimarron Crossing before turning back to the north. When scouts reported an Indian encampment on Pawnee Fork, Anthony was sent to attack with his Fort Lyon troops. Running into a much larger force of Indians than expected, he and his men became surrounded and besieged. Anthony and his men were rescued when Blunt brought his main force up. The Indians retreated, leaving nine dead on the battlefield. Blunt pursued them for two days to the Smoky Hill without success.

Before Black Kettle could reach Fort Lyon, Wynkoop was removed from command there and replaced by Anthony. When the band did arrive in mid-November, Anthony said he could not feed the hungry tribespeople. He recommended that they remain in camp to the north on Sand Creek, where they could hunt buffalo. Black Kettle agreed to do so.

In Denver, meanwhile, Colonel Chivington had enlisted a group of local men as one-hundred-day volunteers of the Third Regiment of Colorado Cavalry. The unit remained inactive until their enlistment had nearly expired, gaining them ridicule as the "Bloodless Third." Chivington was further spurred to make use of the unit by the arrival in

Denver of Gen. Patrick E. Connor. Connor had fought the Shoshones and Bannock Indians in Idaho in 1863 and more recently defeated an Arapaho village on the Tongue River. When he now threatened to attack the Colorado Indians himself, Chivington issued marching orders for the Third Regiment. His aim specifically was to attack Black Kettle's camp on Sand Creek.

On November 24, the unit marched southward along the slopes of the Rocky Mountains through deep snow to the Arkansas River, being joined en route by several companies of the Colorado First Regiment. The garrison at Fort Lyon, unaware of Chivington's plan, was surprised by the arrival of his command on November 28. The officers of the fort, most of whom had ridden with Wynkoop to the Smoky Hill, were dismayed to learn of his plan to attack Black Kettle's camp. Headed by Capt. Silas S. Soule, they expressed their disapproval, saying that to attack the Indians would be to break pledges of safety made to them. This prompted Chivington to walk about the room and declare angrily, "Damn any man who is in sympathy with an Indian!"[3]

Anthony, however, agreed with Chivington and obligingly ordered his Fort Lyon First Cavalry units to fall in with Chivington's command at eight o'clock that same evening to begin an overnight march for Black Kettle's camp. In all, there were nearly seven hundred cavalry troops supported by four twelve-pound howitzers. The small army marched through the night, arriving at dawn at a bend of Sand Creek some forty miles from Fort Lyon. There from the sand bluffs overlooking the site, they could see a hundred or more cross-pole lodges sitting picture-like in the cold, dim light of the winter morning. Pony herds grazed in the distance.

The barking of camp dogs aroused the sleeping village. To show his desire for peace, Black Kettle raised an American flag that had been given him in 1861. Chief White Antelope, who had been at Camp Weld, came from his lodge and ran toward the troops holding his hands high and yelling for the soldiers not to fire. But Chivington did not hesitate. Wanting no surrender from the Cheyennes, he loosed his forces upon the dazed village. Troops were sent galloping to cut the pony herds off from the camp while others joined the artillery pieces in opening fire upon the people who were dashing in panic from their lodges.

In desperation the Cheyennes fled up the marshy, meandering course of Sand Creek, some seeking refuge in crevices and holes along the bank. The troops followed close behind, potshooting any target that presented itself. Frontiersman John Simpson Smith, who was in camp with his Cheyenne wife, described the action:

> The soldiers continued firing on these Indians, who numbered about a hundred, until they had almost completely destroyed them. I think I saw altogether some seventy dead bodies lying there; the greater portion women and children. There may have been thirty warriors, old and young, the rest were women and small children of different ages and sizes.[4]

Somehow Chief Black Kettle and his wife, who suffered several wounds, managed to escape the onslaught. White Antelope was shot down in the creek bed. Another victim was old One-Eye, who had carried Black Kettle's peace overture to Wynkoop. Later when the shooting was over, men of the Bloodless Third murdered Jack Smith, John Smith's blond-headed, half-blood son, while he was sitting quietly in a lodge. His crime was being part Indian. Later his body was tied behind a horse and dragged about on the prairie for a time.

"We, of course, took no prisoners," Major Anthony falsely testified later, "except John Smith's son, and he was taken suddenly ill in the night, and died before morning."[5]

This and numerous other atrocities were revealed later when the army, bending to public outcry, held a hearing on the ordeal in Denver. Congressional hearings were also conducted, but no action was ever taken against any of the military participants. For the Cheyennes and other tribes of the Plains, Chivington's massacre of Black Kettle's village would remain a dire hindrance against placing trust in the word of the white man.

At the same time Chivington was marching toward Sand Creek during November 1864, another U.S. force was pushing eastward down the Canadian River of the Texas Panhandle in search of Indians to fight. Commanding the small army was the well-known mountain man, explorer, and Indian fighter Kit Carson, who now held the rank of colonel of U.S. Volunteers.

Over the years, the Santa Fe Trail had become a favorite raiding place for the southern Plains tribes, who often preyed upon the transportation moving between Missouri and New Mexico. With the Civil War in progress, few U.S. troops were left to serve as escorts and provide protec-

Platte valley east of Courthouse Rock. Though there were few casualties in either of these fights, the war for the Central Plains, ignited by Eayre in western Kansas and inflamed by Chivington at Sand Creek, had become fully engaged.

Books to Read

Berthrong, Donald J. *The Southern Cheyennes*. Norman: University of Oklahoma Press, 1963.

Grinnell, George Bird. *The Fighting Cheyennes*. New York: Charles Scribner's Sons, 1915; Norman: University of Oklahoma Press, 1955.

Hoig, Stan. *The Sand Creek Massacre*. Norman: University of Oklahoma Press, 1961.

Hyde, George. *Life of George Bent*. Norman: University of Oklahoma Press, 1968.

Notes

1. *Missouri Republican*, Nov. 3, 1851.
2. "Sand Creek Massacre," Sen. Ex. Doc. 26, 39/2 (Washington, DC: Government Printing Office, 1867): 217.
3. Ibid., 47.
4. "Massacre of Cheyenne Indians," *Report on the Conduct of the War*, House of Representatives, 38/2 (Washington, DC: Government Printing Office, 1865): 6.
5. "The Chivington Massacre," House of Representatives, Reports of the Committees, 39/2 (Washington, DC: Government Printing Office, 1867): 92.
6. George W. Petis, *Kit Carson's Battle with the Comanche and Kiowa Indians at Adobe Walls on the Canadian River* (Providence: S. S. Rider, 1878), 28–29.
7. Ibid., 22.

CHAPTER FOUR

Sheridan's Men: Clearing Kansas

Following the end of the Civil War in 1865, bitter anger over Sand Creek and the increasing intrusion onto their homeland still burned in the breasts of the Cheyenne Dog Soldiers. Their distrust and suspicions of white people were only increased by the opening of a new stage line along the Smoky Hill River and the thrust of a railroad, the Kansas Pacific, through the very heart of their hunting grounds. On the other hand, the U.S. Government saw the Indian presence in Kansas as a barrier to Western advancement that had to be removed.

During July 1865, a peace council was conducted at the mouth of the Little Arkansas River, now the site of Wichita, Kansas, in an attempt to pacify the Southern Cheyennes and other tribes of the mid-Plains. Despite the presence of such frontier stalwarts as Kit Carson and William Bent, however, most of the Dog Soldiers refused to attend the meeting and continued their attacks on the Platte and Arkansas wagon roads as well as work crews and way stations of the Kansas Pacific Railroad.

During 1866 the United States commenced reforming its Union Army to serve Indian-fighting needs on the Western frontier. Maj. Gen. Winfield S. Hancock was placed in command of the newly designated Department of the Missouri with headquarters at Fort Leavenworth, Kansas. Reorganization of the department's principal offensive arm, the Seventh U.S. Cavalry, commenced at Fort Riley, Kansas, under Lt. Col. George A. Custer, who had won great laurels as a dashing Civil War cavalryman. By the spring of 1867, Hancock felt confident enough to

George A. Custer.
(Custer, *My Life on
the Plains*)

launch an expedition into western Kansas with such a show of force as
to compel the Indians to abandon the warpath.

In late March, Hancock's 1,400-man army marched to Fort Harker
and on to Fort Larned. The force consisted of eleven troops of Seventh
Cavalry riding at the lead of six infantry companies, a battery of
artillery, fifteen Delaware scouts, and a sizable wagon train. Henry M.
Stanley, later to become world famous for his African explorations,
and *Harper's Weekly* artist/correspondent Theodore Davis accompanied the expedition. James Butler (Wild Bill) Hickok served Hancock as
a courier.

Dog Soldier leaders met with Hancock around the fire of his campsite on Pawnee Fork and listened to his demands. But later when the
officer threatened to march on their Cheyenne and Lakota village, their
warriors appeared en masse before the troops. A clash between the
battle-ready Indians and the long line of Seventh Cavalry was barely
averted by now-Indian agent Edward Wynkoop. That night, fearing
another Sand Creek attack, the Indians slipped away to the prairie,
leaving their village standing. Hancock sent Custer and his Seventh

Cavalry in pursuit. But with the trail of the Indians constantly dividing and eventually fading away, Custer gave up and went buffalo hunting.

Hancock, meanwhile, vacillated and finally torched the Indian village, bringing strong criticism on himself from peace advocates for doing so. Custer took his Seventh Cavalry to Fort Hays, resting and replenishing his supplies there until June. Meanwhile General of the Army William T. Sherman developed a plan to call all friendly Indians in to forts along the Platte and attack other hostiles still in the field. In compliance, Custer led six companies of the Seventh on a grueling march northward to Fort McPherson and from there southwestward to the forks of the Republican River. He found no Indians to attack, but early on the morning of June 24 his own camp was engaged by a party of Sioux under Pawnee Killer. A brief parley was held with the chief, but an ensuing pursuit of the band revealed that the heavier cavalry mounts were far too slow for the speedy Indian ponies.

As he had been ordered to do, Custer marched his now famished and exhausted command on to the South Platte River across country severely cut by ravines, spiked with cactus, and baked bone dry by the blazing July sun. At Riverside Station on the Platte, Custer learned by telegraph that he was being sent new orders to report to Fort Wallace on the Smoky Hill River.

During the march to Wallace, Custer's scouts discovered the trail of twelve shod horses that led to a gristly scene. Lt. Lyman Kidder, with ten men and a Lakota scout, had been carrying Custer's new orders from Fort McPherson. Their arrow-spiked remains now lay strewn on the prairie. Custer arrived at Wallace on July 13, having spent 43 days in a fruitless attempt to punish the Indians. In the end, however, it was he who was punished. He was court-martialed for having three of his men shot who had deserted on the trail and for abandoning his post at Fort Wallace in an attempt to meet his wife at Fort Harker. Custer was forced into temporary retirement at his home in Monroe, Michigan.

Even as the Seventh Cavalry had been marching about through northwestern Kansas and eastern Colorado, the Dog Soldiers had continued to raid the work camps and stations of the Kansas Pacific Railroad that was laying rail westward along the Smoky Hill River. On June 21 the Cheyennes attacked a work detail at Fort Wallace. Five days later Capt. Albert Barnitz and Company G of the Seventh Cavalry rode out to rescue workers at Pond Creek Station only to be lured into a trap. He lost six men and had eight others wounded. The abject failure of Hancock and Custer to quell the elusive tribes renewed the demand of the so-called "Olive Branchers" of the day to find a peaceful solution to conflict on the Plains.

Another great peace council was conducted at Medicine Lodge Creek, Kansas, in October 1867. By it the United States hoped to remove the Cheyennes, Arapahos, Kiowas, and Comanches to reservations to the south in Indian Territory and Texas. This time the Dog Soldiers attended and signed the proffered treaty, but only after they had been verbally (and falsely) reassured that it would still be permissible for them to range and hunt in western Kansas. The treaty did nothing to ease the hostility of the Dog Soldiers, who continued their depredations. The worst of these came in August 1868, when a Cheyenne war party raided settlements along the Solomon and Saline Rivers, burning homes, raping women, and taking stock. The United States responded by sending one of its most prominent generals to the region. A bombastic, hard-nosed military leader, Gen. Phil Sheridan quickly searched for a way to strike the Cheyennes. His first two efforts were dismal failures.

One effort involved a group of some fifty civilian scouts under the command of Maj. George A. Forsyth. His second-in-command was a young Lt. Frederick H. Beecher, nephew of the famous New York clergyman, Henry Ward Beecher. The group was buoyed by the mistaken notion that a few well-armed frontiersmen could outfight a much larger body of Indian warriors. Moving to Fort Wallace in far western Kansas, the scouts rashly pushed deep into the Cheyenne-held badlands cut by the Kansas-Colorado border despite alarming signs of Indian presence.

On the evening of September 16, they camped on the Arikaree Fork of the Republican River, having crossed the Kansas line into Colorado. They were awakened the following morning by the sentry's cry of "Indians! Indians!" At that moment several Cheyenne warriors rushed the scouts' horses and waved blankets in an attempt to stampede them. A barrage of gunfire now erupted from a large body of other Indians who surrounded the camp.

Taken completely by surprise, the scouts made a dash for a sandbar in the river where some trees and sandbanks offered protection, leaving their pack mules and camp goods behind. Their situation was precarious at best. Forsyth was the first to be wounded, one shot striking him in the right thigh and another shattering a bone in his left leg. He was dragged to safety by Dr. John H. Moors, who in doing so was struck by a bullet in his forehead. Moors would die after lying mortally wounded for three days. Later Lieutenant Beecher was hit by a shot that severed

Phil Sheridan.
(*Leslie's Illustrated Newspaper*)

his backbone. He suffered through great agony until at sundown he finally expired.

Led by their famous war chief Roman Nose, the Cheyennes made several assaults against the sandbar positions. The embattled scouts were able to hold the Indians at bay. During one charge, however, Roman Nose was hit as he jumped his horse over a scout's rifle pit during a charge. Mortally wounded, he rode back to his camp, where he died the next morning.

The Cheyennes kept the scouts pinned down for nine days and killed all of their horses before finally withdrawing. A relief column arrived to find the small command in desperate condition, having no medical supplies for their wounded and only their dead horses for food.

At the same time Forsyth and his scouts were in the field, another Sheridan-directed effort was being made against the Indians in northwestern Indian Territory. Under the command of Brig. Gen. Alfred Sully, a large military expedition marched south from Fort Dodge, Kansas. It consisted of nine companies of Seventh Cavalry, under Maj. Joel Elliott, and one company of infantry. Reaching the conflux of Beaver and Wolf Creeks that form the North Canadian River, the expedition found itself harassed by taunting warriors who stood on their ponies at a distance and thumbed their behinds at the soldiers. Sully attempted to attack the Indians; but with his wagons becoming mired in the sandy hills and scant hope of effectively engaging the Indians, he turned his army about and returned to Dodge. He claimed to have killed twenty-two Indians, but this number was totally unsupported. His losses were three dead, including a trooper who had been captured as he lagged behind at a campsite and was carried off by the Indians.

Beset by these failures, Sheridan concluded that the only way to defeat the Indians was to catch them in their camps during cold weather. Accordingly, he laid plans for a multipronged winter campaign that would hit the Indians from several directions. One advance would be made from Fort Lyon, Colorado, under Maj. Eugene A. Carr; another from Fort Bascom, New Mexico, under Col. A. W. Evans; and a third, composed principally of the Seventh Cavalry, would march south from Kansas. To command the Seventh, Sheridan pulled strings for the return of the exiled Custer, who had retired to his home in Michigan following his recent court-martial.

The huge train of wagons, infantry, cavalrymen, and scouts departed Fort Dodge on November 12, 1868, and moved to the Beaver-Wolf Creek conflux. There a supply camp was constructed and preparations made for Sheridan's winter strike against the Indians. An early snowstorm struck Camp Supply on the evening of November 22. Custer had already ordered his Seventh Cavalry troops to prepare for a march, and the snow further delighted him. Now it would be easy to follow the tracks of anyone who ventured out across the wilds of northwestern Indian Territory. It was still snowing hard when early the next morning the call "To Horse" sounded. The Osage guides and white scouts led the way with the band close behind. With the collars of their buffalo coats turned high to protect them and their instruments from the driving snow, the band played the popular marching song, "The Girl I Left Behind Me." The long double column and the expedition's forage wagons moved southwestward up Wolf Creek, making their first camp fifteen miles south of Camp Supply after fording Wolf Creek. The fording place near present Fargo, Oklahoma, would become known as Custer's Crossing.

An artist's concept of Custer's attack at Washita. (Dodge, *Our Wild Indians*)

Cobb, which Sheridan had designated as a sanctuary for friendly Indians. When the Cheyenne leader had asked for asylum, however, he was rejected by Gen. William B. Hazen, who said he could not speak for Sheridan. Now, as Custer's men engulfed his camp, both Black Kettle and his wife were shot from the back of their horse as they attempted to flee eastward across the river. The two fell dead in the icy waters of the Washita.

The few Cheyenne warriors fought back as best they could, but they were overwhelmed by the mounted troops who swept through the village and pursued victims into the snowy fields. The attack soon became dispersed into individual actions.

By midmorning Custer had his victory. Over a hundred Cheyennes had been killed, and fifty-three women, young girls, children, and babies had been taken prisoner. Before torching the fifty-one captured lodges, Custer had his men gather their contents: saddles, bridles, lariats, bows and arrows, shields, spears, rifles, revolvers, buffalo robes, hatchets, clothing, and the camp's winter supply of dried buffalo meat, flour, and other vital provisions. After souvenirs had been taken, these items were also burned. But the most severe material loss to Black Kettle's people was the 875 Cheyenne ponies that were rounded up and shot on Custer's orders.

Four troopers had been killed during the charge, the most notable among them being Capt. Louis Hamilton, grandson of Alexander Hamilton. Capt. Albert Barnitz was shot by a youthful warrior after the initial charge but survived. The greatest loss among the Seventh Cavalry occurred when Major Elliott led a random group of seventeen men on a chase eastward up the Washita in pursuit of some fleeing Indians. In doing so, they became surrounded by warriors from other Cheyenne and Arapaho camps downstream and were annihilated to a man.

With no knowledge of what fate had befallen Elliott and the men with him, Custer abandoned the battlefield during the afternoon and hurried back to Camp Supply to report his victory to Sheridan and send dispatches detailing his victory to Eastern newspapers. The bodies of Elliott and his men were not found until a military expedition under Sheridan and Custer returned to the battle site on December 11.

Also found on the battleground at that time were the bodies of Mrs. Clara Blinn and her baby son, who had been held captive and were killed during the attack. Elliott's men were buried along the Washita, while the bodies of the officer and the two Blinns were sent to Fort Arbuckle and eventually on to permanent burial sites.

Sheridan and Custer continued on down the Washita toward Fort Cobb. En route they were met by a large body of mounted Kiowas under Satanta, Lone Wolf, and Kicking Bird. Satanta and Lone Wolf were taken captive and placed in chains at Fort Cobb pending the surrender of their people. During December Sheridan sought a location for a new military post closer to the raiding paths into Texas. As a result Fort Sill was found-ed at the base of the Wichita Mountains.

Sheridan returned to Kansas in February 1869. A month later Custer led the Seventh Cavalry and a regiment of Nineteenth Kansas Volunteers on their return, detouring into the Texas Panhandle to search for two Kansas women known to be captives of the Cheyennes. After a trying march to the Red River, Custer picked up an Indian trail that led him northward along the 100th meridian. His thirsty and bone-weary troops were strung out in disorder when he came onto Chief Medicine Arrow's Cheyenne village on the Sweetwater River.

Luring three Cheyenne men to his camp, Custer took them hostage against the release of the two white women. The pair, dressed only in gunny sacks, were eventually brought forth. With them and the three Cheyenne captives in tow, Custer marched back to Camp Supply and on to Fort Hays, Kansas, leaving Fort Sill and the Plains

Indians under the control of Col. Benjamin Grierson and his Tenth Cavalry buffalo soldiers.

The other arms of Sheridan's campaign had been active as well. At the same time that Sheridan and Custer were marching south from Kansas into Indian Territory, Maj. Eugene A. Carr led twelve troops of cavalry and one of infantry southeastward from Fort Lyon into the Texas Panhandle. For two months he hunted the Canadian River without finding any Indians to fight. His greatest enemy was the fierce winter storms that swept the open prairie. With his supplies badly used up, Carr advanced no farther than his supply base west of Adobe Walls, returning to Fort Lyon on February 19 with nothing to show for his march.

On November 18, 1868, Maj. Andrew W. Evans drove eastward down the Canadian River from Fort Bascom, New Mexico, with a 454-man expedition comprised of Third Cavalry and Thirty-seventh U.S. Infantry. After establishing a supply depot on Monument Creek near the Antelope Hills, he scouted the region for Indians. When an Indian trail leading north to south beyond the Antelope Hills was discovered, Evans set off in pursuit. The trail led him past the headwaters of the Washita River to the North Fork of the Red River, where signs and distant sightings of Indians increased among the rugged canyons of the region. On December 22, a winter storm drove the command to the protection of a bluff overhang, but on the following day Evans pushed ahead along the snaking river.

Contact with the Indians occurred on December 25 when an advance detachment under Maj. E. W. Tarlton became engaged with a large party of warriors. The Indians charged the troops with rifles, pistols, and lances. Evans' troops repulsed the charge and drove the Indians back downriver to where their village was situated below a high cliff. He then brought up his artillery and shelled the village, causing its frightened occupants to flee. The Indian defenders took up rifle positions among the rocks on the ridges above. Still the troops were able to take the village, which they later learned was a Comanche encampment of some sixty lodges under Chief Horse's Back. Among the material captured were large quantities of foodstuff in addition to camp necessities and personal items.

At this point, another force of mounted Indians, wearing their war bonnets and displaying their weapons in defiance, appeared on the heights of the opposite bank. These were Kiowas under Chief Woman's Heart. They contented themselves with harassing Evans' command with rifle fire as it advanced on downstream and, on one occasion, fired the grass in front of the troops. Evans lost only one man during the engagement. Though the ground was bloody in places, the Indian loss was not known.

With his horses badly jaded, Evans began his return march. On December 30 the Fort Bascom troops were met twenty miles east of Fort Cobb by four scouts who informed them of Custer's Washita fight. Upon receiving supplies from Sheridan at Fort Cobb, Evans returned to his subdepot on Monument Creek and from there marched back to Fort Bascom.

Of the three arms of Sheridan's winter campaign, only the one under Major Carr had failed to engage the Indians and thereby win battle laurels. Caught in the grasp of winter on the open plains, he floundered around in the Texas Panhandle and failed to advance beyond the Canadian River. Carr had distinguished himself during the Civil War, attaining the rank of brevet major general, and he was jealous of the national fame as an Indian fighter that Custer had won at the Washita.

But fate would ultimately reward him with a battle victory that followed from Sheridan's invasion of the Indian Territory. While some bands of Cheyenne came into Camp Supply and surrendered, there were others under control of the recalcitrant Dog Soldiers who had held to their old hunting grounds north of the Arkansas River in western Kansas and eastern Colorado. One of these was that of Dog Soldier chief Tall Bull. Having been one of the few Dog Soldier leaders to sign the Treaty of the Little Arkansas in 1865, Tall Bull was infuriated by General Hancock's burning of the Cheyenne village on Pawnee Fork and returned to war against the whites in Kansas.

"I was blind with rage," he told the peace commissioners at the Treaty of Medicine Lodge, "and what I have done since then I am not ashamed of."[1]

During the spring of 1869, a number of Sioux and some Arapaho joined Tall Bull's band on the headwaters of the Republican River, bringing his camp to some eighty-four lodges. The men of Tall Bull's camp hunted the buffalo herds that still inhabited the region. They also resumed their raiding habits, striking white transportation along the Platte and Smoky Hill Rivers. To protect these roads, Carr and his Fifth Cavalry command were moved from Fort Lyon to Fort McPherson near present North Platte, Nebraska. Adding some fifty Pawnee scouts under Maj. Frank North and scout Buffalo Bill Cody to his eight troops of Fifth

Cavalry, four hundred strong, Carr set out on an Indian-hunting expedition on June 9, 1869.

Marching southwestward to the Republican River, Carr followed it to the Arikara Fork in Colorado. There, near the Beecher's Island battle site, his Pawnee scouts picked up a fresh trail of a sizable Indian camp. This would prove to be that of Tall Bull, who had decided to move north across the Platte to join the Sioux proper.

Upon reaching the South Platte near a trail point known as Summit Springs, Tall Bull had found the river running high from spring rains. He camped there to wait until the stream subsided and, with the buffalo plenty, allow his warriors to do some hunting. Carr caught up with him there on July 11.

The joint charge of Carr's cavalry and the Pawnee scouts took the camp by surprise. Though the panic-stricken villagers fled in all directions, seeking what cover they could find, they were cut down without regard to sex or age. Tall Bull himself was killed along with fifty-two others. The troops looted the camp, then torched it and the remaining contents. Some four hundred horses and mules were rounded up and driven back to Sedgwick.

Two white women, German immigrants who had been captured on the Saline River on May 30, had been held prisoner in the camp. One of these was slain during the attack, but the other survived her wounds and was rescued.

Carr's victory over Tall Bull effectively ended the Cheyenne Dog Soldiers' dominance over western Kansas and eastern Colorado. But, despite Custer's crushing of Black Kettle's village, there was still another war to be fought for the Southern Plains.

Books to Read

Chalfant, William Y. *Cheyennes and Horse Soldiers: The 1857 Expedition and the Battle of Solomon's Fork*. Norman: University of Oklahoma Press, 1989.

Custer, Elizabeth. *Boots and Saddles*. Norman: University of Oklahoma Press, 1962.

Custer, George Armstrong. *My Life on the Plains*. Norman: University of Oklahoma Press, 1968.

Greene, Jerome A. *Washita, the U.S. Army and the Southern Cheyennes*. Norman: University of Oklahoma Press, 2004.

Hoig, Stan. *The Battle of the Washita*. New York: Doubleday, 1976; Lincoln: University of Nebraska Press, 1979.

Nye, W. S. *Carbine and Lance: The Story of Old Fort Sill*. Norman: University of Oklahoma Press, 1943.

Utley, Robert. *Frontier Regulars: The United States Army and the Indian, 1866–1890*. New York: Macmillan Publishing Company, 1973.

Note

1. *Cincinnati Commercial*, Nov. 4, 1967.

Kiowa chief Kicking Bird.
(Battey, *Life and Adventure*)

Among them were the wife and two children of Afro-American Brit
Johnson. A year later, the determined Johnson appeared at the mouth of
the Little Arkansas where commissioners were holding a treaty council
with the Kiowas and others. He said that he had just redeemed his wife
and two children from the Comanches, ransoming them with horses.
The commission party managed to rescue some of the other captives as
well, but there were others still being held by bands that had learned the
ransom value of children and women.

One such infraction against Texas settlers was the 1866 murder of
James Box and the capture of his wife and three daughters in Montague
County as they were returning home in a wagon following a visit to rel-
atives. In July 1870, a large Kiowa-Comanche war party led by Kiowa chief
Kicking Bird swept though Jack and Montague Counties in Texas, looting
and stampeding cattle. Two drovers were killed and one captured before
the raiders were intercepted on the Little Wichita River west of present
Seymour by Capt. Curwen McLellan and fifty-six Sixth Cavalry troopers

Kiowa Chief Satanta.
(Custer, *My Life on the Plains*)

from Fort Richardson. The Indians killed three of the troopers and wounded twelve others in the fight.

In January 1871 a Kiowa war party slew four Black teamsters near Weatherford, Texas. Another raid occurred on May 18 when a Kiowa party led by Satanta and Mamanti ambushed a train of freight wagons at Salt Creek Prairie on the wagon road in present Young County, Texas, between Forts Richardson and Griffin. Seven of the teamsters were killed and mutilated.

General of the Army William T. Sherman and a small entourage had passed by the massacre site on an inspection tour of frontier forts only a short time before. Later at Fort Sill, upon learning the identity of the perpetrators, he ordered the arrest of Satanta, Satank, and warrior Big Tree. Elderly Kiowa chief Satank was killed when he attempted to escape from the wagon in which he was being taken away.

Satanta and Big Tree were tried for murder at Jacksboro, Texas, and sent to prison at Huntsville.

A far-ranging Kiowa war party under Big Bow attacked a munitions wagon train at Howard Wells near present Big Springs, Texas, killing seventeen Mexican teamsters in April. A Ninth Cavalry patrol from Fort Concho caught up with the Indians and attacked them, losing an officer and an enlisted man in the ensuing fight.

A joint expedition conducted north of the Red River by Col. Ranald Mackenzie from Fort Richardson and Col. B. F. Grierson from Fort Sill during August proved fruitless. Mackenzie returned again in October only to have the Quahada Comanches attack his camp and steal some seventy mounts. His Fourth Cavalry troops pursued the raiders onto the Staked Plains but were forced to turn back when a blizzard struck.

Mackenzie fought the Quahadas again in September 1872 when he struck their camp on McClellan Creek in the Texas Panhandle. He destroyed 262 lodges while killing 23 Indians and capturing 120 to 130 women and children along with some 3,000 horses and mules.

The Southern Cheyennes, too, were growing more and more unruly. On March 18, 1873, a Cheyenne war party fell on the surveying camp of E. N. Deming, killing him and three of his assistants. Open warfare flared during the summer of 1874 when a joint war party comprised mainly of Cheyennes, Comanches, and Kiowas attacked Adobe Walls, where a party of buffalo hunters had ensconced themselves in the ruins of the old trading post. By a stroke of good fortune, hunter Billy Dixon was awakened early and alerted his companions. They repulsed the Indian charge, and with their long-range buffalo guns eventually drove the attackers from the field.

Fearing a widespread outbreak, Cheyenne and Arapaho agent John D. Miles at Darlington Indian agency fled up the Chisholm Trail to Kansas with his agency staff. On the way he came onto the charred remains of freighter Pat Hennessey, who had been tied to a wagon wheel and burned to death. Hennessey's three teamsters had also been killed. The Cheyennes struck still another party of surveyors below Fort Dodge on August 26, an incident known as the Lone Tree Massacre. These depredations brought an immediate response from Phil Sheridan, now commanding the Division of the Missouri. He was determined to break the backbone of Indian resistance in Indian Territory. His new military campaign involved an invasion of western Indian Territory and the Texas Panhandle by five separate columns. Gen. Nelson Miles would drive

Nelson Miles.
(Miles, *Personal
Recollections*)

southwest from Camp Supply; Maj. William Price eastward from Fort
Union, New Mexico; Col. Ranald Mackenzie north from Fort Concho,
Texas; Col. J. W. Davidson, west from Fort Sill; and Lt. Col. George Buell
north from Fort Griffin, Texas.

Even as the operation was getting under way, a big fight erupted at
the Wichita agency, located to the north of Fort Sill on the Washita River.
Hostile elements of the Kiowas under Satanta—who had been released
on the promise of the Kiowas' good behavior—Lone Wolf, and others
had taken their bands there in hopes of sharing in the annuity issues of
the Wichitas, Caddos, and other bands. When the Kiowas began looting
the Wichitas' corn cribs and melon fields, a plea for military help was
rushed to Fort Sill. Davidson responded with four troops of Tenth Cavalry
buffalo soldiers.

On August 22 Davidson attempted to disarm Kiowa subchief Red
Food. But the Kiowa rebelled. Red Food jumped on a horse and fled with

troops firing at him. He was not hit, but a general melee and riot ensued. Several people were killed, and buildings were burned before additional Fort Sill troops arrived to quell the disturbance. Many of the hostiles now fled toward the Staked Plains of the Texas Panhandle and the sanctuary of the Palo Duro Canyon.

During mid-August, Miles led eight companies of Sixth Cavalry and four of Fifth Infantry, plus thirty-nine scouts and guides from Supply, down Wolf Creek and turned south to the Canadian River. A forward scouting party under Lt. Frank Baldwin, Fifth Infantry, skirmished with a party of Indians at Adobe Walls and another on the Canadian with minor results. Miles continued on southward to the Sweetwater.

When he was attacked by a large Cheyenne war party, Baldwin countered and drove the Indians southward to the brakes of the Red River. There they disappeared into the recesses of Palo Duro Canyon, though Miles managed to destroy one abandoned Indian village. With his supplies and forage exhausted, Miles swung about and returned north to the Washita where he established a supply depot pending further operations.

On September 9, a large force of Kiowas attacked a thirty-six-wagon train carrying rations from Camp Supply to Miles's camp. Capt. Wyllys Lyman and his escort of some fifty Fifth Infantry soldiers desperately held off the attackers for six days but were kept under siege until relief forces arrived from Camp Supply.

During this time, on September 12, another party of Kiowas attacked four soldiers and two scouts, Billy Dixon and Amos Chapman, who were on their way to Camp Supply with dispatches from Miles. The six took refuge in a buffalo wallow and held the Indians at bay until a cold rain caused them to retire. One soldier was killed, and Chapman later lost a leg from a wound he received in the fight.

Price's column was also in the same area, having marched south from the Canadian River before turning north along the 100th meridian. His Navajo scouts found and attacked an Indian village on Gageby Creek southwest of the Antelope Hills. The villagers escaped, but Price destroyed the lodges, food supply, and other necessities of life. During October, Buell, who had killed ten Comanches on Double Mountain Fork, Texas, during a January expedition, was successful as well. He and his mounted Eleventh Infantry invaded present Greer County, Oklahoma, attacked tribal camps, and burned several hundred lodges.

The combined bands of Cheyennes, Kiowas, Comanches, and others who had taken refuge in the Palo Duro mistakenly thought they were safe

Frank D. Baldwin.
(Miles, *Personal
Recollections*)

after Miles had withdrawn. They were soon to be discovered on the canyon floor, however, by Seminole and Tonkawa Indians scouting for Mackenzie with his eight companies of Fourth Cavalry and five of Tenth Infantry. On the morning of September 28, Mackenzie's cavalrymen led their horses down the steep walls and launched a surprise attack on the joint village, taking it in a rout. Though few Indians were killed, Mackenzie captured and burned some four hundred lodges along with their food supplies and equipage. This loss, plus the 1,414 ponies and mules that Mackenzie captured and slaughtered, did much to destroy the Indians' ability to resist further or remain aloof from their agencies during the coming winter.

One of the most dramatic engagements of the entire campaign came on November 8 as Lieutenant Baldwin with a troop of cavalry and a company of Fifth Infantry was escorting a train of twenty-three empty supply wagons back to Camp Supply from the Staked Plains of the Texas Panhandle. En route along McClellan Creek, Baldwin's scouts discovered the camp of Cheyenne chief Grey Beard. Baldwin, who would win a second Medal of Honor for his action in the affair, loaded his infantry riflemen aboard the empty wagons and, with the cavalry on the flanks, charged the village. The surprised camp was driven out onto the prairie, leaving behind two young white girls, Adelaide and Julia Germain, who along with two older sisters had been captured on the trail in western Kansas following the massacre of their family.

Davidson, marching west from Fort Sill up the North Fork of the Red River, pursued Grey Beard without success during September. On October 21 the Fort Sill commander led a second expedition to Elk Creek where three of his Tenth Cavalry troops under Maj. G. W. Schofield surprised and captured a Comanche camp consisting of 69 warriors and 250 women and children in addition to some 1,500 to 2,000 horses. Davidson's command pushed on west to McClellan Creek in the Texas Panhandle. A unit of his command under Capt. C. D. Viele picked up the trail of Grey Beard's flight from Baldwin's attack and pursued it for 96 miles. Several skirmishes ensued with the Cheyennes' rear guard, and a number of ponies and mules were captured. But the expedition was ended when a fierce, zero-degree norther drove the Indian-hunting expedition back to Fort Sill.

On November 28, Charles A. Hartwell and four companies of Eighth Cavalry under Price's command attacked a band of forty or more of Grey Beard's warriors on Muster Creek of the Texas Panhandle, driving them into the Palo Duro. Then on December 1, 1st Sgt. Dennis Ryan and twenty Sixth Cavalry troopers attacked and pursued a band of Indians on Gageby Creek, capturing fifty ponies and personal goods.

Another Fort Sill strike was conducted by Capt. A. B. Keyes and buffalo soldiers of Troop I, Tenth Cavalry, in December. Marching north to the head of Kingfisher Creek, Keyes and his men captured thirteen warriors and their families whom they turned over to a military unit stationed at the Darlington Cheyenne-Arapaho agency on the North Canadian. Keyes then followed the trail of another Cheyenne band some eighty miles up the North Canadian, eventually capturing the group of fifty-two Indians and seventy ponies on December 28.

The viciously cold weather continued into early 1875, forcing the starved, desperate bands to begin surrendering. Notable among the Kiowa hostiles giving up at Fort Sill were Lone Wolf, Mamanti, and Woman's Heart. Satanta, who had been hiding out in the Red Hills along the North Canadian following the Wichita agency fight, gave up himself and his small band to Lt. Col. Thomas H. Neill at Darlington. He was quickly sent on to Fort Sill and from there back to prison at Huntsville. On February 27, 1875, Cheyenne chief Stone Calf surrendered to Neill, releasing the two older Germain girls, Catherine Elizabeth and Sophia Louise. Neill described the event:

> The Indian warriors with their bronzed and scarred countenances, silent, respectful, and thoughtful,—the young men and boys with an expression between fear and shame; the women with their babes under their arms, hiding the heads of the children under their blankets to prevent them from seeing the white man, who they had been taught to fear as their worse enemy; the parti-colored blankets and leggings; the tepis or lodges behind them, and the trees in rear of all, presented a scene at once grand, important and unequalled, and which we shall never see again.[1]

The Red River campaign was over, but the fighting was not. The government had decided that some of the hostiles would be sent to prison at St. Augustine, Florida. During the chaining of the Cheyennes who had been selected at Darlington near present El Reno, Oklahoma, a warrior named Black Horse attempted to escape and was shot down. A melee ensued, with the Cheyennes taking up a defensive position in the sand hills along the river. There they held off troops under Neill with weapons that they had hidden before surrendering. Six Cheyennes were killed, and nineteen soldiers wounded. That night the Indians escaped by wading through a pond during a rainstorm.

Many of the Cheyennes eventually returned to the agency, but some continued on north with the aim of joining the Northern Cheyennes. On April 23, 1875, one of these bands led by Little Bull was discovered and attacked on the Middle Fork of Sappa Creek in northwestern Kansas by a troop of Sixth Cavalry from Fort Wallace. The soldiers, commanded by Lt. Austin Henely, surrounded the small band and killed some twenty-seven men, women, and children. Henely lost two men in this culminating encounter with the Southern Plains Indians.

As a result of the Red River War, Fort Elliott in the Texas Panhandle and Fort Reno in the Indian Territory just south of the Darlington agency were created, joining Fort Sill and Camp Supply in overseeing the Indians of the region. Texas' principal concern with the tribes now involved the driving of Texas longhorns up the Chisholm and other cattle trails to Kansas markets across tribal lands of the Indian Territory. Miles and Mackenzie and the forces under them would now be called north to contest the Sioux and Northern Cheyennes.

Books to Read

Battey, Thomas C. *The Life and Adventures of a Quaker among the Indians.* Norman: University of Oklahoma Press, 1968.

Carriker, Robert C. *Fort Supply, Indian Territory: Frontier Outpost on the Plains.* Norman: University of Oklahoma Press, 1970.

Chalfant, William Y. *Cheyennes at Dark Water Creek.* Norman: University of Oklahoma Press, 1997.

Haley, James L. *The Buffalo War: The History of the Red River Indian Uprising of 1874.* Garden City, NY, 1976. Reprint, Norman: University of Oklahoma Press, 1985.

Hoig, Stan. *Fort Reno and the Indian Territory Frontier.* Fayetteville: University of Arkansas Press, 2000.

———. *The Kiowas and the Legend of Kicking Bird.* Boulder: University Press of Colorado, 2000.

Hutton, Paul Andrew. *Phil Sheridan and His Army.* Lincoln: University of Nebraska Press, 1985; Norman: University of Oklahoma Press, 1999.

Leckie, William H. *The Buffalo Soldiers: A Narrative of the Negro Cavalry in the West.* Norman: University of Oklahoma Press, 1967.

McConnell, H. H. *Five Years a Cavalryman, or, Sketches of Regular Army Life on the Texas Frontier, 1866–1871.* Norman: University of Oklahoma Press, 1996.

Miles, Nelson A. *Personal Recollections and Observations.* New York: The Werner Company, 1896.

Note

1. Neill to AAG, Dept./Mo., March 7, 1975, LR/Dept. Mo., NA.

CHAPTER SIX

Red Cloud's War:
Contests of the
Northern Plains

The Teton Sioux Indians and their Northern Cheyenne allies were a powerful force on the Northern Plains. The largest of three divisions of the Sioux Nation, the Tetons consisted of seven loosely confederated tribes known as the Oglala, Brulé, Hunkpapa, Miniconjou, Sans Arc, Two Kettle, and Blackfeet. An upright and spirited people, it was not surprising that they would have strong, resolute leaders to oppose U.S. domination of their lands. Red Cloud was one. Others would emerge during their long contest with the United States, among them Crazy Horse, Gall, Spotted Tail, and Sitting Bull.

The first serious though disorganized challenge by the Sioux to white domination occurred in Minnesota during 1862. Trouble erupted on August 17 when some renegade braves killed four white men and two women after being refused food and whiskey. The situation soon flared into a full-scale, seven-day war wherein Sioux raiding parties massacred some 737 men, women, and children. Four hundred of the warriors were tried and condemned to death. President Lincoln pardoned most of the prisoners, but thirty-eight of the Sioux leaders were executed by hanging.

Most of the two thousand Sioux who were still in the field fled to Dakota Territory. Gen. Henry Sibley was sent up the Missouri River after them, and on July 14, 1863, he routed a large Sisseton (Santee Division) Sioux hunting party in present Kidder County, North Dakota, killing thirteen. Still another U.S. force under Gen. Alfred Sully attacked some

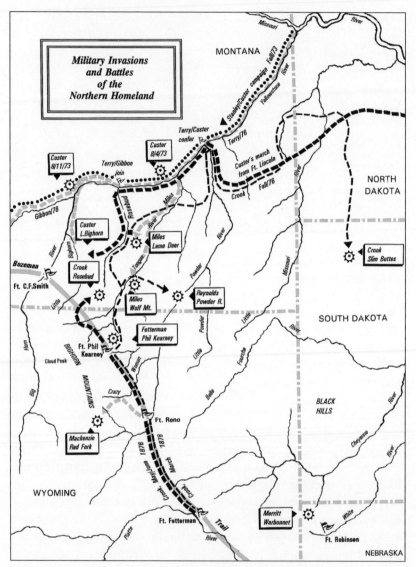

Military invasions of the Northern Homelands. (Courtesy of author)

sixteen hundred Yanktonai (Yankton division) and Hunkpapa Sioux at Killdeer Mountain, North Dakota, on July 28. In a bloody thirty-minute fight, Sully's forces killed over a hundred of the Dakota Sioux, took 158 prisoners, destroyed 500 lodges, and made off with a large number of ponies, buffalo meat, and robes. Then on September 3 and 4, Sully engaged a village of some four thousand Santee and Teton Sioux at White Stone Hill, North Dakota, killing another 150 Indians, taking more prisoners, and burning their village. These defeats forced many of the dissident bands to return to the reservation.

Other bands of the Sioux, meanwhile, were contesting U.S. ascendancy on the Central Plains. On April 16, 1864, Brulé chief Spotted Tail met with Gen. Robert B. Mitchell at Fort McPherson (then Fort Cottonwood). During their talks, Spotted Tail adamantly rejected demands that the Sioux stay away from the Platte Trail. Not only that, he wanted the new stage road along the Smoky Hill River, their best buffalo country, closed. And, he warned, if surveyors were not withdrawn from the Niobrara in present Nebraska they would be killed. It was not the Platte Road, however, that incited the Sioux to all-out war. Another trail leading off northwestward from the Platte at Fort Laramie to the silver mines of Montana cut through the very heart of the Oglala Sioux and Northern Cheyenne homelands. Whites called it the Bozeman Trail after gold-seeker John Bozeman, who opened the route.

The post–Civil War contest for the North Country was ignited with a bloody engagement at the Platte River bridge at present Casper, Wyoming, on June 25, 1865. During the preceding spring, the Sioux and Northern Cheyennes had been harassing troops and transportation on the Platte Trail. The already volatile relations between whites and Indians were exacerbated by the actions of Col. Thomas Moonlight, commander at Fort Laramie. When two Sioux men arrived at the fort to return a captive white woman and child they had ransomed, the hard-drinking Moonlight ordered the Indians hanged in artillery trace chains and left to rot in public view.

The tribes, still enraged by Chivington's attack at Sand Creek, held a joint war council and laid plans for conducting war along the Platte Road. The place chosen for an initial attack was the soldier stockade that guarded the bridge spanning the Platte River. A well-organized force of some two thousand Sioux, Cheyenne, and Arapaho warriors took positions in the hills overlooking the bridge and prepared for the attack. First, a small decoy of men was sent down to show themselves and attempt to draw the soldiers out from the fort. This ploy failed when the troops were too wary to follow for any distance.

A short fight ensued, however, when the Indians struck a party of soldiers who were seen approaching the fort. These soldiers carried word to the fort that a train of five supply wagons was on its way in. Apparently the train was oblivious to the current Indian threat. Lt. Caspar Collins, son of General Collins who had just arrived at the fort, volunteered to take a troop forth and provide escort for the train. When the Indians saw the soldiers ride out across the long bridge, it was precisely what they had wanted.

One party of warriors was sent galloping down to cut the soldiers off from the fort, while another blocked them at the front. Entrapped, Collins and his twenty-five men had little chance against the massive force of warriors. Seeing their plight, the troops turned and fought their way back to the fort. Under support of cannon fire from the fort, some of them made it to safety. Eight men including Collins, however, were knocked from their saddles and killed. Collins himself was struck in the forehead by an arrow. His body was later found wrapped in telegraph wire, his hands and feet were cut off, and his heart and tongue cut out.

In other attacks along the trail, the Indians killed seventeen people and took two girls, ages six and two, captive. In an effort to chastise the recalcitrant tribes, Gen. Grenville M. Dodge, commanding the Department of the Missouri, ordered a military strike into the Powder River country of Wyoming. Gen. Patrick E. Connor, who was placed in command of the campaign, established a post on the Powder, which he named Camp Connor. On August 11, he moved north from there with an army of 675 troops. During the march, his Pawnee scouts pursued and annihilated a group of twenty-four Cheyennes believed to have been party to the Platte bridge attack. Then on August 29 at the Tongue River, Connor's Pawnee scouts discovered an Arapaho village under Chief Black Bear. Connor attacked, driving the Indians upstream. After capturing the village, Connor burned the lodges and camp equipage along with the bodies of dead villagers. Nearly a thousand horses and mules were taken. The Arapahos harassed the troops as they withdrew and managed to recapture some of their animals.

Another arm of Dodge's invasion under Col. N. Cole suffered disastrously from bad weather, rough terrain, lack of Plains experience, and attacks by both the Northern Cheyennes and Sioux. While moving up the Powder River, Cole lost large numbers of horses, wagons, and supplies. Many of his mounts died from hunger and cold when carelessly left on the picket line in severe weather. To keep them from the Indians, Cole burned his wagons, harnesses, saddles, and other equipment. When finally rescued by Connor's Pawnee scouts, the command of some eighteen hundred ragged, dismounted cavalrymen was in a state of near

Fetterman Massacre Monument. (Photo by author)

starvation. Connor was held responsible, perhaps unfairly, for the utter failure of Cole. He was relieved of his command, and his forces withdrawn from Wyoming.

The army soon returned, however, when the Sioux and Northern Cheyennes began conducting strikes along the Bozeman Trail. In June 1866 Col. Henry Carrington arrived at Fort Laramie with seven hundred construction troops of the Eighteenth Infantry under orders to construct two new forts along the Bozeman. During a meeting with Sioux leaders, Carrington was warned by Oglala chief Red Cloud that if the white chief came with soldiers to steal the road, he would have to fight.

From Fort Laramie, Carrington marched north to Crazy Woman's Fork, where he upgraded Camp Connor and renamed it Fort Reno. Despite continued objections from the Sioux and Northern Cheyennes, Carrington pushed ahead with the building of Fort Phil Kearny in north-central Wyoming and Fort C. F. Smith on Montana's Bighorn River.

Not long after he arrived at the Fort Phil Kearny site, Carrington received a message from Northern Cheyenne chief Black Horse. The chief asked if he had come for peace or war. Carrington responded with an invitation for Black Horse to meet with him. On July 16, the Cheyennes arrived en masse to be greeted by Carrington and his officers in their dress uniforms and gala airs from the infantry band. In council, the

Cheyennes lost no time in telling Carrington that they wanted the road into their country stopped.

"What are you doing in this country, anyhow?" they asked. "You come here and kill our game; you cut our grass and chop down our trees; you break our rocks [conduct mining], and you kill our people. This country belongs to us, and we want you to get out of it."[1]

Carrington was not deterred. He continued with the erection of his forts. He soon found, however, that his construction troops were no match for Sioux and Northern Cheyenne raiders who ravaged trains along the Bozeman and attacked soldier details sent to gather logs for building the forts. They also ran off stock from the army camps, and it became increasingly dangerous for anyone to venture forth from the posts. The Fort Phil Kearny garrison, equipped with old muzzleloading muskets numbering less than four hundred strong, was ill-prepared to defend itself.

During October the Indians attacked a wood detail near Fort Phil Kearny and killed two men. Again, on December 6 the Indians laid siege to another wood-gathering detail from the fort. Carrington attempted to entrap the attackers, but before escaping back to the fort he ended up with an officer and a sergeant being killed. The Indians came again on December 19. When sent in pursuit, Capt. James Powell wisely refused to go beyond Lodge Trail Ridge where the Indians had set a deadly trap.

The wood train came under attack once more on December 21. Despite specific orders not to do so, Capt. William J. Fetterman let himself, along with three officers, seventy-six troops, and four civilians, be drawn beyond the ridge. There they were quickly surrounded by some fifteen hundred warriors under Sioux leader Red Cloud and Northern Cheyennes under Dull Knife and Little Wolf. Fetterman and his command were wiped out to the last man in what was the worst defeat suffered by the Indian-fighting army to that date. It is thought that Fetterman and another officer committed suicide by shooting one another. All of the victims were stripped of clothing and their bodies mutilated.

Red Cloud and his Oglalas continued to conduct war along the Bozeman Trail. Another wagon train was attacked near Fort Phil Kearny on August 2, 1867. But this time, the results were much different. Armed with new .50 caliber Springfield rifles and well supplied with ammunition, the soldiers took up positions behind their overturned wagons and cut down one charge after another. When some sixty of his warriors were killed, Red Cloud began to realize that the white man could not be driven away. From that point on, Red Cloud became a peace advocate.

Red Cloud. (Dunn,
*Massacre of the
Mountains*)

The U.S. Government also realized its military incapacity to protect the transportation and migration that had begun moving onto and across the Plains at the end of the Civil War. Officials now sought to make new peace alliances with the tribes. During April and May 1868, U.S. commissioners met with the Sioux and Northern Cheyennes at Fort Laramie, securing agreements whereby the tribes would go to assigned reservations but retain the right to roam and hunt the buffalo so long as there was ample game. This brought a temporary interlude of peace on the Northern Plains, but trouble would soon return.

Still another avenue of intrusion of the North Country, the Northern Pacific Railroad, was constructed during the 1870s, bringing even more military posts and U.S. troops. Sioux leaders all firmly opposed government efforts to relocate their people on a Missouri River reservation in the Dakotas, far distant from their hunting grounds in Wyoming and Montana. This opposition was exercised both in visits to Washington, DC, and by strikes against mining camps, railroad surveyor crews, settlements, and wagon transportation.

The gauntlet had been thrown. Neither the Sioux nor the government would back away from the stark potential of war. During the fall of 1873, a military expedition commanded by Col. David S. Stanley, supported by the Seventh Cavalry under Custer, drove up the Missouri and Yellowstone Rivers by land and steamboat in an attempt to quell the Sioux raiders. In doing so that August, Custer and his men twice engaged the Sioux, once at the Tongue and again near the mouth of the Bighorn River—a stream that he would revisit three years later with dire consequence. The three-month incursion up the Yellowstone to the Musselshell River served only to incite the infuriated Sioux to even greater resistance.

This situation worsened considerably during 1874 when Custer led an expedition into the Black Hills, a heavily forested region that both the Sioux and Northern Cheyennes claimed with particular passion. Supposedly the purpose of the expedition was to locate a site for a new military post, but it served to open still another region of the West to a frenzy of gold seekers. With Sioux leaders resisting all efforts by the United States to purchase the Black Hills region, and with government authorities being unwilling to remove the miners and other settlers who had entrenched themselves there, the Indian Bureau issued an edict on December 6, 1875. Either the Sioux would go to their reservations and live peacefully or troops would be sent to subdue them. Having signed the 1868 agreement at Fort Laramie, Red Cloud no longer led the Sioux resistance to white intrusion, but other strong leaders had taken his place. Most notable among them were his nephew Crazy Horse and another unrelenting foe of white domination named Sitting Bull.

Books to Read

Bourke, John G. *On the Border with Crook.* New York: Charles Scribner's Sons, 1891; reprint: Glorieta, NM: Rio Grande Press, 1971.

Brown, Dee. *Fetterman Massacre.* Lincoln: University of Nebraska Press, 1962.

Carrington, Margaret. *Absaraka: Home of the Crows, Being the Experience of an Officer's Wife on the Plains*. Lincoln: University of Nebraska Press, 1983.

DeMallie, Raymond J., ed. *The Sixth Grandfather: Black Elk's Teachings Given to John Neihardt*. Lincoln: University of Nebraska Press, 1984.

Finerty, John F. *War-Path and Bivouac, or, The Conquest of the Sioux*. Chicago: M. A. Donohue & Co., 1890. Reprint: Norman, University of Oklahoma Press, 1961.

Hyde, George E. *Red Cloud's Folks: A History of the Oglala Sioux Indians*. Norman: University of Oklahoma Press, 1968.

Kime, Wayne R. *The Black Hills Journal of Colonel Richard Irving Dodge*. Norman: University of Oklahoma Press, 1996.

King, Charles. *Campaigning with Crook and Stories of Army Life*. New York: Harper & Brothers, 1890.

Larson, Robert. *Red Cloud: Warrior-Statesman of the Lakota Sioux*. Norman: University of Oklahoma Press, 1999.

McDermott, John D. *Frontier Crossroads: The History of Fort Caspar and the Upper Platte Crossing*. Casper: Fort Caspar Museum, 1997.

Olson, James. *Red Cloud and the Sioux Problem*. Lincoln: University of Nebraska Press, 1978.

Paul, Eli, ed. *The Autobiography of Red Cloud*. Helena: Montana Historical Society, 1997.

Sandoz, Mari. *Crazy Horse, the Strange Man of the Oglala Sioux*. Lincoln: University of Nebraska Press, 1992.

Utley, Robert M. *Frontiersmen in Blue: the United States Army and the Indian, 1845–1865*. New York: Macmillan Publishing Co., 1967.

———. *The Indian Frontier of the American West, 1846–1890*. Albuquerque: University of New Mexico Press, 1984.

Vaughn, J. W. *Indian Fights: New Facts of Seven Encounters*. Norman: University of Oklahoma Press, 1966.

Note

1. George A. Woodward, "Some Experiences with the Cheyennes," *United Service* 1 (April 1878): 194.

CHAPTER SEVEN

Desperate Pursuit: Shadow of the Little Bighorn

Hearkening to the success of his winter campaigns of 1868 and 1874 against the southern tribes, Sheridan was determined to hit the Sioux quickly in 1876 before spring when the Indians would be even more difficult to catch. Once again he laid plans for a multipronged thrust into Indian-held country. Gen. Alfred H. Terry would strike west up the Yellowstone from Fort Abraham Lincoln on the upper Missouri. Gen. George Crook would lead an expedition northward from Fort Fetterman in Wyoming. And Gen. John Gibbon at Fort Ellis, Montana, would drive eastward down the Yellowstone. But Sheridan's hope for an early strike was not to be.

The northern winter with its heavy snows impeded the delivery of supplies and equipment and the arrival of the new recruits that Terry badly needed at Fort Abraham Lincoln in present North Dakota. Further, the man he greatly desired for field commander, Custer, was being detained in Washington, DC, by President Ulysses S. Grant, who was angry with him over testimony he had given to Congressional committees.

In Wyoming, despite the winter conditions, Crook managed to get his military expedition organized and push up the Bozeman Trail from Fort Fetterman on March 1. His command consisted of two companies of Fourth Infantry, five of Second Cavalry, and five of Third Cavalry, with Col. Joseph J. Reynolds as field commander. By the time Crook's army reached Crazy Woman's Fork, however, a blizzard struck.

George Crook.
(*Appleton's Cyclopedia
of American Biography*)

Parking his wagons, Crook pushed on up the Tongue River in the face
of gale-force winds, heavy snow, and bitter cold. When two Indians
were spotted, Reynolds and a cavalry force trailed them eastward to
the Powder River. There the troops discovered a village of some one
hundred lodges.

Believing the village to be that of Crazy Horse, Reynolds attacked,
driving the villagers into the hills and capturing their herd of some six to
eight hundred ponies. Four soldiers were killed in the attack, and six
wounded. Reynolds torched the village, which proved not to be Sioux
but a Northern Cheyenne camp under Old Bear. That night the
Cheyennes returned and recaptured their horse herd. Charging that
Reynolds had been inept in conducting the operation, Crook turned
about and returned to Fort Fetterman to await more temperate weather
before returning to his campaign.

Crook's army gathers at Fort Fetterman. (*Leslie's Illustrated Newspaper*)

It was May 17 before Terry embarked from Fort Abraham Lincoln with his Sioux-hunting expedition, his main engagement force being seven hundred Seventh Cavalry under Custer. These twelve troops along with three companies of infantry and the mule-drawn supply wagons marched overland, following the muddy banks of the Heart River to the Yellowstone. Terry himself boarded the steamship *Far West*, which carried the expedition's supplies up the longer river route. On June 21 the two legs of the expedition consolidated at the head of the Powder River. There Custer boarded the steamer to confer with Terry and Gibbon, whose six companies of Seventh Infantry, four of Second Cavalry, and twenty-five Crow Indian scouts were still en route down the Yellowstone.

On a large map aboard the steamer, the three men studied the area south of the Yellowstone where the scouts had reported seeing smoke. A plan emerged for Custer to march to the head of the Rosebud and then swing back northward up the Little Bighorn and attack any Indians he found there. Gibbon, meanwhile, would advance southward down the Bighorn and block retreat in that direction, thus entrapping the Indians in the valley of the Little Bighorn.

Crook, in the meantime, had set off again from Fort Fetterman, now with a reorganized command consisting of ten troops of Third Cavalry, five of Second Cavalry, and five of Fourth and Ninth Infantry. Lt. Col. William B. Royall commanded the cavalry, and Maj. Alexander Chambers the infantry. Because of the limited communication of the day, there was a complete lack of contact and coordination of effort between Crook and Terry.

Alfred H. Terry.
(*Leslie's Illustrated
Newspaper*)

Crook again marched up the Bozeman to beyond the Tongue River, where he established a large base camp on Goose Creek at the site of present Sheridan, Wyoming. On June 16, after being joined there by 262 Crows and Shoshones, he parked his wagon train and pushed more directly north to the Rosebud valley where he believed Crazy Horse was camped. The command was taking a morning rest when it suddenly came under a fierce attack from Sioux and Northern Cheyenne warriors. A hard-fought battle ensued for some six hours before the attackers were finally driven off.

Crook later claimed victory in the fight, but in addition to losing a large number of men killed and wounded, Crook's portion of Sheridan's campaign was stopped short. He returned to Goose Creek and made no further advance against the Indians until the following fall. As a result, his forces were unavailable to support Custer in his epic battle that occurred eight days later only some thirty miles from his Rosebud battle site.

At the time of Crook's fight, Maj. Marcus Reno of Custer's command was reconnoitering some forty miles to the north. In reaching the Rosebud, Reno had exceeded orders, causing Terry great concern that the Indians may have been alerted to the presence of troops. As a result, Custer was ordered to march to the head of the Rosebud, bypassing a trail that led off west to Little Bighorn, and advance on the Indians from the south.

Like Reno, Custer did not follow Terry's orders. Pushing up the west bank of the Rosebud, he came to the trail on the evening of June 24. Instead of continuing on south, this indication of Indian presence was too tempting for him. He turned west on the trail with intentions of resting his wearied command on the dividing ridge between the Rosebud and Little Bighorn. But when scouts reported an Indian encampment only a few miles ahead in the valley beyond and fearing that his column had already been discovered, Custer made a fatal error of judgment. He chose to push ahead with his attack without waiting for Gibbon to arrive in place.

To a large extent, Custer's Indian-fighting experience had been one of frustration over the Indians' reluctance to stand and fight in the style of white combatants. The main task, he and his officers concluded, was catching them. They were confident that once the Indians were entrapped they could be defeated. It would prove to be a tragic miscalculation.

With the huge Sioux-Northern Cheyenne encampment still not in sight when he crested the divide, Custer initiated his plan of attack. Capt. Frederick Benteen was dispatched with three troops of the Seventh Cavalry on a scout off to the left of the column. Custer continued to follow the Indian trail toward the Little Bighorn. When they encountered some Sioux warriors to the left across what is now known as Reno Creek, Custer ordered Reno to charge them with three troops, 112 men, of the Seventh.

Reno and his men plunged off in pursuit, crossing the creek and then the Little Bighorn. He did not realize that his force was attacking the south end of a huge encampment, and he and his men were sorely unprepared for the fierce resistance they would meet. Sioux warriors swarmed to the defense of their village, forcing Reno to dismount his cavalrymen as skirmishers. The heavy barrage of Indian fire soon drove the troops into a precarious retreat. In less than an hour Reno's command suffered forty-seven men killed and fifty-three wounded and was

One of the many versions of the Battle of the Little Bighorn depicting Custer as the last man to die at the Little Bighorn. (Newsom, *Thrilling Stories Among the Indians*)

rendered so ineffective as to no longer pose a threat whatever to the Indians or offer effective assistance to Custer.

Reno would claim later that Custer had promised him support in his action. Instead, however, Custer marched off to his right with five troops of the Seventh, 215 strong, leaving one troop behind to guard the pack train. Benteen had still not returned to the main command from his scout. Custer sent a courier galloping to him with orders to hurry forth with ammunition packs. Clearly, Custer's intention was to swing around the encampment and attack the Indians from the north while Reno engaged them on the south. But there were serious flaws in this thinking in terms of both terrain and enemy strength.

The encampment of Sioux and Northern Cheyennes was far larger and stronger than ever expected, its warrior force numbering well over fifteen hundred, possibly as many as four thousand. Moreover, the Indians were well armed, many with repeating rifles, and the warriors were fully primed for a big fight. Having plunged into battle without making any estimate of his foe, Custer had also failed to consider the lay of the ground upon which he fought. In traversing the elevated east bank of the Little Bighorn, his march was impeded by the rugged hills and ravines of the high ground that elongated and delayed his advance. This gave the Indians ample time to pull back from their engagement with Reno and concentrate on Custer's approach.

Sioux and Northern Cheyenne fighting men massed at the river crossing leading into the village at its center. Their fire power soon drove Custer's men up from the river onto the east ridge above. Mounted warriors poured up behind the troops, cutting them off from any retreat back to their comrades. Custer retreated to a knoll of the ridge, and his famous last stand there was brief, deadly, and complete. Custer and every last man with him perished on that hot afternoon of June 25, 1876.

Because there were no survivors, the mystery of precisely how the battle developed and what happened will never be known with certainty. It is known that it was close to 3 o'clock in the afternoon when Custer and his immediate command advanced northward along the east bluffs of the Little Bighorn. Whether or not he followed Medicine Tail coulee down to the river crossing and was halted there has been the subject of much speculation.

It is altogether apparent, however, that Custer and his men were soon forced on north to the battlefield site. There they dismounted and took up defensive firing positions against an overwhelming number of Sioux under Chief Gall abetted by Northern Cheyenne warriors. Sioux pictographs indicate the cavalry horses were stampeded away, leaving Custer's men afoot and, apparently, desperately hoping that Benteen would arrive with the ammunition packs and supportive manpower.

Benteen had arrived at the bluffs adjacent to Reno when the latter's fractured and demoralized command was dragging itself back across the Little Bighorn. Still under enemy fire, Reno ordered both units to dig rifle pits and, though the sound of heavy firing could be heard from the direction Custer had taken, he refused to send support. When some of his officers attempted to go forward, they were driven back by mounted warriors. The remnant Seventh Cavalry remained in position under heavy siege from Indian riflemen through the remainder of the twenty-fifth and throughout the day of the twenty-sixth.

Even as that long, hot day began, the embattled troops under Reno and Benteen had been without water for the past twenty-four hours. This increased the suffering for all of the troops, but especially for the wounded. "The sun beat down on us," Pvt. Jacob Adams later wrote, "and we became so thirsty that it was almost impossible to swallow."[1]

At great risk, a few volunteers made a dash to the river and obtained enough water for the wounded. In doing this, Pvt. Mike Madden lost his

Sioux Chief Gall.
(Walker, *Campaigns of Custer*)

leg after it was shattered by an Indian bullet. The crippled remnant of Seventh Cavalry remained in position under siege until the morning of June 27 when Terry and Gibbon arrived from the north and the Indians withdrew. "I never saw anything in all my life," Pvt. Edward Pigford declared, "that looked as good to me as Terry's men."[2]

The strewn, stripped, and often mutilated remains of Custer and his men were temporarily buried on the field of battle where they had fallen. Later the bodies of Custer and the other officers were taken to Fort Leavenworth for burial. Custer's defeat had cast a pall over a nation that was then engaged in a celebration of its Centennial.

Crook, meanwhile, had waited at the Goose Creek camp for Col. Wesley Merritt to arrive from Fort Laramie with the Fifth Cavalry. Merritt and his unit were delayed, however, by an engagement on July 17. Merrit had learned

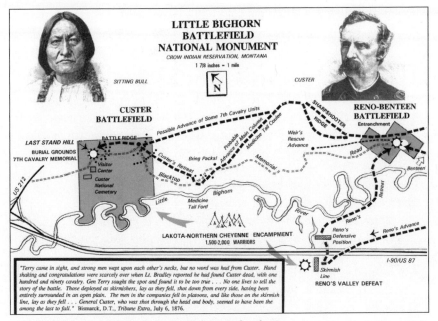

Little Bighorn Battlefield scenario. (Courtesy of author)

that some eight hundred Northern Cheyennes had left Red Cloud Agency on the White River with the intention of joining the hostiles who had defeated Custer. A hasty march led to Merritt's interception of the Indians on War Bonnet Creek in far northwestern Nebraska. The Cheyennes dispersed without a fight after "Buffalo Bill" Cody killed a Cheyenne subchief named Yellow Hair. Cody scalped his victim, claiming it to be the "first scalp for Custer."

Crook took to the field again on August 5. Five days later on the Rosebud he unexpectedly met Terry's army moving south. The two commands joined and made a muddy, fruitless march eastward to the Powder River. There in disgust Terry turned back to the Yellowstone, while Crook continued on in his search for Indians to the Little Missouri and Heart Rivers until his rain-drenched command became so destitute for food that they were eating their played out horses. Finally Crook turned south for the Black Hills mining towns for supplies.

Capt. Anson Mills, guided by scout Frank Grouard, was sent ahead with 150 men of the Third Cavalry to obtain rations. On September 8, at a place known as Slim Buttes in northwestern South Dakota, Mills's detachment came onto a Sioux camp of thirty-seven lodges under Chief

American Horse. As Custer had done at the Washita, Mills waited through the night and attacked the camp at dawn under a cold, foggy rain. He captured the camp, but the Sioux fought back with sniper fire from a wooded ravine.

Having used most of his ammunition, Mills sent a courier galloping off to Crook, who arrived at the captured village shortly before noon with a detachment of Merritt's Fifth Cavalry. The soldiers poured salvo after salvo into the ravine, killing several Sioux including some women and children and eventually forcing out the others. Among them was American Horse, who had been shot in the stomach. Attempts to save him failed, and he died during the night. A number of Sioux women and children were also among the casualties.

Crook's men looted the village and found a wealth of foodstuff and goods along with a Seventh Cavalry guidon, saddles, orderly books, and other artifacts of Custer's defeat. Late in the afternoon, Sioux and Cheyenne warriors from a nearby camp arrived to counterattack, but Crook's men held them off as the soldiers pushed on toward the Black Hills. The command suffered the loss of three dead and twelve wounded, among the latter being Lt. Adolphus H. von Leuttwitz, who had been shot in the knee during the opening charge and suffered the amputation of his leg.

Shortly after Terry's departure, new forces had arrived on the Yellowstone by steamboat: six companies of Twenty-second Infantry under Lt. Col. Elwell Otis and six of Fifth Infantry commanded by Gen. Nelson Miles. Miles, a self-promoting but capable officer, established a cantonment at the mouth of Glendive Creek and prepared for a campaign against the Sioux. Marching north he personally met with Sitting Bull at Cedar Creek, north of the Yellowstone, on October 20. But when the Hunkpapa Sioux leader would not bend to demands that he take his people to the reservation, Miles attacked. The "Walk-a-heap" infantry troops doggedly pursued the band south and east, forcing it to abandon much of its food supply and equipage before Miles finally lost its trail.

Though elements of the Miniconjou, Oglala, and Sans Arc Sioux surrendered, Sitting Bull remained out. In December Miles took up the chase again. On the seventh, Lt. Frank Baldwin and a force of Fifth Infantry found Sitting Bull at the head of Redwater Creek and captured 122 lodges. Sitting Bull and his band again escaped, however.

Even as Miles pursued the Sioux north of the Yellowstone, Crook was preparing for another thrust northward from Fort Fetterman with an even larger force. This consisted of eleven troops of cavalry under Col. Ranald Mackenzie and fifteen companies of infantry under Lt. Col. R. I. Dodge. Additional fighting strength came from some four hundred Indian allies from various tribes. Maj. Frank North commanded the Pawnees, while Lt. William Philo Clark led the remainder.

Crook again marched up the Bozeman Trail to old Fort Reno, which now functioned as a supply base. After waiting out a blizzard there, Crook was brought word of a large Cheyenne encampment located to the west in the Bighorn Mountains. Mackenzie was sent to find and attack the village.

With ten troops of cavalry and the large contingent of Indian allies, Mackenzie pushed up Crazy Woman's Fork and south to the Red Fork of the Powder River. On the frosty morning of November 25, Mackenzie's force arrived at the entrance to a large, bowl-shaped valley that held the Northern Cheyenne camp, whose principal men included Dull Knife and Little Wolf. After pausing briefly to organize his attack, Mackenzie sent his forces, Indian allies at the lead, charging down on the village.

Cheyenne scouts had reported that there were white soldiers on the way. But a recent victory over some Shoshones had roused the defiance of the Cheyenne war element. A nightlong war dance was dwindling to an end when the attack came, and the few who were still awake sounded the alarm. As the villagers dashed from their lodges and fled for the surrounding hills, the warriors took up defensive positions among the rocks and ravines. From there they responded to Mackenzie's onslaught with a barrage of determined rifle fire that blunted the charge on the North Fork's badly cut bank above the village.

In leading his company of cavalrymen across a ravine, 1st Lt. John A. McKinney was shot from below and killed, causing the four-abreast troopers behind him to pile onto one another in disarray. For a time the cavalry charge was stymied along the line of the ravine across which the two forces exchanged fire and at times battled in hand-to-hand combat.

The Pawnees, meanwhile, had swept into the evacuated village and on through to capture a horse herd at the far end of the valley. Eventually the Cheyennes were driven off into the snowy hills, with scant clothing and no food or horses. A good many of the refugees froze to death while others managed to straggle to the Tongue River camps of Crazy Horse.

In their deserted camp, the troops found more evidence of participation in the Custer battle. Mackenzie ordered the village burned and, after giving some of the captured seven hundred ponies to his Indian allies, had the remainder shot. The event was an enormous disaster for the Northern Cheyennes, one that ultimately would drive them to surrender.

Crook continued his march north to scour the Belle Fourche country and that of the lower Little Missouri River. Again he had no success in ferreting out the Sioux. His command suffered through blizzards with temperatures ranging to fifty degrees below zero until finally in December Crook called an end to the campaign and sent his military units back to their home bases.

Miles, however, refused to let the severe Montana weather impede his operations. In early January, with bitter cold and with knee-deep snow on the ground, he led five companies of Fifth Infantry and two of the Twenty-second south from his cantonment to the head of the Tongue River. As he neared Wolf Mountain, he was attacked by some five hundred Cheyenne and Sioux warriors under Crazy Horse.

With his two pieces of field artillery, Miles held off the Indians until a driving blizzard brought an end to the fighting. The Indians withdrew, and Miles turned back to his base near the Yellowstone. Though little had been achieved in the effort other than the capture of a party of Cheyenne women and children, Miles opined to General Sherman, an uncle of his wife, that he had clearly outdone Crook.

During the spring of 1877, competition arose between Miles and Crook in their efforts to persuade the tribes to surrender. When Crook sought to entice them into the Red Cloud agency at Camp Robinson, Miles sent a Cheyenne captive woman and a mixed-blood scout to the Northern Cheyenne-Sioux camps on the Little Bighorn. As a result of this, several bands of the Northern Cheyenne surrendered to Miles, their warriors enlisting as scouts with him. But others, principally Dull Knife, Little Wolf, and Turkey Leg, along with Sioux bands under Crazy Horse, surrendered at Red Cloud. Sitting Bull, however, took his Miniconjous north to Canada.

Another group of Miniconjous under Lame Deer refused to surrender. Hearing that he had gone to the Rosebud to hunt, Miles led a combined force of cavalry and infantry in search of the dissident Sioux. On May 7, Miles found Lame Deer's camp and directed a charge on it by units of the Second Cavalry. In the ensuing fight, the Sioux suffered fourteen killed while Miles lost four troopers. Lame Deer himself was shot and killed by an officer when he attempted to surrender to Miles personally. Though their village was destroyed and their horse herd captured, the Sioux band regrouped under Lame Deer's son, Fast Bull. Miles kept after the band for the remainder of the summer until finally in September Fast Bull surrendered at Spotted Tail Agency.

Crazy Horse was stabbed to death by another Sioux at Camp Robinson on September 5, 1877, when he resisted an attempt to place him under arrest. Later that month, a Sioux delegation led by Red Cloud and Spotted Tail visited Washington, DC. There they were promised reservations at Spotted Tail and Pine Ridge agencies in present South Dakota.

At this time another major Indian crisis developed, one that would begin in the mountains of Oregon but ultimately spread east to Montana and involve the Indian-fighting forces there. In October 1877, efforts of a peace commission to persuade Sitting Bull to return to the United States ended when the Sioux leader declared that he did not want to hear any more lies.

The government eventually forced most of the Sioux nation to reservations in present South Dakota, at the same time establishing a strong military presence at forts along the upper Missouri and Yellowstone Rivers. Miles's cantonment in Montana, being joined by Fort Custer near the site of Custer's defeat, became Fort Keogh. Sherman totally rejected efforts by the ambitious Miles to follow Sitting Bull across the Canadian border where the intractable Sioux leader held to his Canadian refuge.

Even as Sitting Bull remained in Canada, another oppressed tribe of the Northwest was making a heroic attempt to achieve a similar exodus from U.S. control. Though the Nez Percé were of Sahaptin lineage and resided in the mountainous Snake River country of Idaho and Oregon, they were strongly affected by Plains Indian culture, commonly crossing the Rockies to hunt the buffalo plains. In 1875 the government reneged on its commitment to let the Nez Percé band under Chief Joseph remain on their Wallowa Valley homeland of Oregon in favor of white settlement. Though sorely tempted to go to war, the Nez Percé accepted their unjust fate and made ready to join others of their tribe on the Clearwater Reservation in Idaho. While making the move, however, three of their young men who were fired up on whiskey killed four white men who had given them trouble. Other killings followed.

This set U.S. forces under Gen. O. O. Howard in pursuit of the Nez Percé through the rugged ranges of the Salmon River Mountains and began one of the epic chapters of the U.S. Indian Wars. After a month's weary march, Joseph's band rested, safely, they believed, in the Big Hole Basin of western Montana. But a 200-man force under Col. John Gibbon engaged them by surprise, routing the camp. The Nez Percé regrouped, pinned Gibbon down in a wooded area, and fought him to a standstill until a relief force under General Howard arrived. Casualties were heavy on both sides—70 for Gibbon, 87 for Joseph—before the Nez Percé retreated into Idaho. Pursued by Howard, Joseph's warriors valiantly fought off U.S. troops as they fled across Idaho, Wyoming, and Montana in a desperate bid to reach Canada. As they moved across what is now Wyoming's Yellowstone National Park, the army command laid plans to block them. Col. Samuel Sturgis and six companies of Seventh Cavalry took up positions on Clark Fork, which flowed northward to the Yellowstone River, while Col. Wesley Merritt and his Fifth Cavalry held the easterly flowing Stinking Water.

The Nez Percé outmaneuvered Sturgis and slipped northward toward what is now Billings, Montana. Making a forced march, Sturgis caught up with the band beyond the Yellowstone River at Canyon Creek. There the Nez Percé warriors effectively fought off Sturgis and escaped on to the north. Now Gen. Nelson Miles at Fort Keogh was called on as a last resort in preventing the escape of Chief Joseph and his people. Commanding a sizable force of cavalry, infantry, artillery, and Northern Cheyenne and Sioux scouts, Miles caught up with the band at Snake Creek in Montana's Bear Paw Mountains on the morning of September 30. The Nez Percé, thinking they were well ahead of the pursuing troops, had paused to let their badly worn and weary people rest only some forty miles from Canada.

Miles attacked immediately, capturing the band's vital horse herd while losing a number of key officers and noncoms to the selective fire of the Nez Percé defenders. An impasse ensued for five days before Chief Joseph, realizing the futility of continuing the struggle, came to Miles and spoke his famous words of surrender:

"Hear me, my chiefs! I am tired. My heart is sick and sad. From where the sun now stands, I will fight no more forever."[3]

Books to Read

Buecker, Thomas R. *Fort Robinson and the American West, 1874–1899.* Lincoln: Nebraska Historical Society, 1999.

Greene, Jerome A. *Slim Buttes: An Episode of the Great Sioux War.* Norman:

University of Oklahoma Press, 1982.

Hebard, Grace Raymond, and E. A. Brinnistool. *The Bozeman Trail.* 2 vols. Lincoln: University of Nebraska Press, 1990.

Hedren, Paul L. *First Scalp for Custer: The Skirmish at Warbonnet Creek, Nebraska.* Lincoln: University of Nebraska Press, 1987.

———. *Fort Laramie and the Great Sioux War.* Norman: University of Oklahoma Press, 1988. Originally titled *Fort Laramie in 1876: Chronicle of a Frontier Post at War.*

Schubert, Frank N. *Buffalo Soldiers, Braves, and the Brass: The Story of Fort Robinson, Nebraska.* Shippensburg, PA: White Mane Publishing Co., 1993.

Smith, Sherry. *Sagebrush Soldier: Private William Earl Smith's View of the Sioux War of 1876.* Norman: University of Oklahoma Press, 1989.

Stewart, Edgar L. *Custer's Luck.* Norman: University of Oklahoma Press, 1955.

Utley, Robert M. *The Lance and the Shield: A Life and Times of Sitting Bull.* New York: Yale University Press, 1963.

Vaughn, J. W. *Reynolds' Campaign on the Powder River.* Norman: University of Oklahoma Press, 1961.

Ware, Capt. Eugene F. *The Indian War of 1864.* New York: St. Martin's Press, 1960.

Notes

1. *Entrenchment Trail*, brochure, Custer Battlefield National Monument (Montana: National Park Service, 1961): 6.
2. Ibid., 18.
3. Robert Utley, *Frontier Regulars* (New York: Macmillan Publishing Co., 1973), 314.

Cheyenne leaders Little
Wolf and Dull Knife.
(Smithsonian Museum
of Natural History)

being told to return to their agency, the Cheyennes firmly declined, saying they would fight first. Warriors began disappearing into the adjacent ravines.

At this point, with no order from Rendlebrock to do so, Lt. A. E. Wood, who had arrived from West Point only a few days before to take charge of Troop H at the rear of the march, ordered his men to fire; and the fight began. The troops soon found themselves surrounded and under attack by the Cheyennes. Heavy firing continued through the day with two soldiers being killed.

By far the worst enemy for the Fort Reno troops was the scorching sun and the lack of water for either the men or their animals, their last camp having been at a pool whose stagnant, salt-laced water had made several of the men ill. Canteens had not been refilled. Firing ceased at dark, but the Cheyennes did not go away during the night. At daybreak,

Cheyenne camp on North Canadian River near Fort Reno. (Western History Collection, University of Oklahoma)

with ammunition running low, Rendlebrock's officers all agreed that the command's situation was precarious and it should retreat to water.

The retreat quickly became a rout, with the Cheyennes aggressively pursuing the distraught troops. One trooper was knocked from his saddle by a Cheyenne bullet, but the command was in such disarray that nothing was done to save him. Once the command reached a spring, Little Wolf's warriors finally withdrew, and the next day the Fort Reno command limped on west to Camp Supply. There, much to their distress, they were quickly ordered back to their pursuit.

The Cheyennes continued their trek north into southern Kansas, scavenging the fenceless ranch country for horses and supplies and killing several ranchmen along the way. They were met again in Clark County, Kansas, by a troop of Fourth Cavalry from Camp Supply under Capt. William C. Hemphill. The Cheyennes defended themselves from the brush and cutbacks along Sand Creek and held off the troops, causing them to fall back to Fort Dodge. Two days later, a composite force under Rendlebrock caught up with the Indians again, this time on upper Sand Creek.

Once again the Indians set up a strong rifle position that Rendlebrock concluded was too dangerous for his men to charge. He contented himself with following on the Cheyennes' trail to the Arkansas River. There the command was bolstered by two troops of cavalry from Fort Elliott, Texas, under Capt. Clarence Mauck. Lt. Col. William B. Lewis of Fort Dodge took overall command as the pursuit continued on northward.

Lewis was at the lead of his columns when they entered the valley of Punished Woman's Fork north of present Scott City, Kansas, on September 27. He had dismounted his men for a brief midafternoon rest when Little Wolf's men launched a sudden attack, sending his warriors charging down from the bluffs in a well-planned ambush. The surprised troops fled in panic to the surrounding bluffs. Once there, however, Lewis and his officers were able to organize a skirmish line and advance on foot toward a box canyon on the opposite side of which the Cheyennes had established rifle positions.

In an effort to urge his troops forward across the barren bluffs that offered them little protection, Lewis rode ahead to the edge of the chasm. When his horse was shot in the flank, he dismounted. Soon after he himself was hit by a Cheyenne bullet that severed the femoral artery in his thigh. With Lewis incapacitated, Mauck now took charge of an inconclusive rifle battle across the ravine. At dark he withdrew the troops and horses to the protection of a dry wash leading into Punished Woman's Fork and waited out the night.

Mauck had reasoned that the Cheyennes were entrapped in their ravine and could not escape. But he was wrong. When morning came, they were gone. Mauck destroyed sixty-two Cheyenne horses left behind and set off in pursuit. Lewis was sent to Fort Wallace with an escort, but he died en route.

One Cheyenne was found dead on the battlefield. No one knew just how many warriors had been killed, but their loss of horses and accouterments was heavy. This fact may have contributed to the havoc and mayhem that took place as they advanced through the farming communities along the Solomon River, Prairie Dog Creek, Sappa Creek, and Beaver Creek. Farm houses were ravaged, stock taken, men and boys were killed, and women were raped.

Mauck and his troops witnessed the destruction as they trailed the Cheyennes toward the Platte River of Nebraska. At the same time, other army units had taken to the field in an effort to stop the Cheyennes. The Indian entourage had slipped past infantry troops stationed along the Kansas Pacific Railroad under Col. Richard I. Dodge. And troops from Fort Wallace, sent out by Gen. Jefferson C. Davis (not the Confederacy president), arrived on the Beaver too late to intercept the determined band.

Similarly, the army's effort to establish a barrier along the Union Pacific rail line at the Platte River proved inept. A locomotive under steam stood ready at Sidney, Nebraska, to rush troops under Maj. Thomas T. Thornburgh forward. But still Thornburgh's force arrived at Alkali Station too late to intercept the band as it crossed the line and disappeared into the sand hill country of western Nebraska.

Accompanied for a time by Mauck's worn and weary command, Thornburgh pursued the Cheyennes into the sand hills but soon lost the trail. He then pushed on north to the Snake River, where he joined forces with a Third Cavalry search force under Maj. Caleb H. Carlton from Camp Robinson. The combined columns marched on to Camp Sheridan, never seeing anything more of the Cheyennes.

Once beyond the Platte River and into the sand hills, the Cheyennes split into factions under Dull Knife and Little Wolf. The former wished to return to the Red Cloud Agency, not knowing that while he was in Indian Territory it had been moved from Camp Robinson to the Dakotas. Little Wolf, however, was cautious about going to the agency and chose to remain in hiding in the Nebraska sand hills during the winter.

An early winter's storm had struck the area on October 22 when Capt. John B. Johnson with a detachment of Third Cavalry and Sioux scouts encountered Dull Knife's ragged band coming down Chadron Creek in northwestern Nebraska. Though still prepared to fight to the death, the freezing and starved band was finally persuaded to surrender and be taken to Camp Robinson.

At Robinson the Northern Cheyennes were held in an abandoned barrack, fed, and treated well for a time. But the government remained determined that they should be returned to Indian Territory. The Cheyennes were equally determined that they would not go back south—they would die first, they said again and again.

Finally in early January 1879, government authorities pushed the matter to a crisis. Capt. Henry W. Wessells Jr., who had become commander of what was now "Fort" Robinson, undertook severe measures. He ordered that fuel, food, and water be withheld from the imprisoned Cheyennes until they submitted to removal back to Indian Territory. Still Dull Knife's Cheyennes remained unswervingly adamant; they would die before they would return. Their young warriors, fearing punishment for crimes in Kansas, took charge in the barracks. Ripping up the floor, they retrieved the few weapons they had hidden there and barricaded the windows with blankets and boards.

Then at about ten o'clock on the frozen night of January 9, they led a break for freedom.

The escape began with shots fired from the window of the barracks at the guards walking their posts. Immediately after, warriors plunged through the windows to grab up the rifles of the killed or wounded sentinels. When the sound of gunfire brought soldiers in their long underwear swarming from their quarters, five Cheyennes formed a rear guard for the stream of tribespeople as they fled through the snow toward the White River.

The five warriors were soon either killed or badly wounded. The soldiers, led by Wessells, fired at any dark form moving across the field of snow. Men, women, and children alike fell under the rain of bullets. Those who survived the dash to the river struggled through the icy waters and snow to the bluffs that towered to the northwest of the post. There many of them were killed or captured by mounted cavalry coming up from a camp below Fort Robinson. A small group of warriors and women carrying babies made it to the top of the bluffs. This party, led by warrior Little Finger Nail, would elude the Fort Robinson troops for twelve days as the Cheyenne party fled northwestward through the pine-decked hills.

There was still no surrender in the Cheyennes, and several soldiers were killed in encounters en route to Coliseum Butte, a towering plateau that overlooked a level plain through which Hat Creek drained northward. It was only when the Cheyennes slipped off the butte and moved north up Antelope Creek that the troops finally cornered them in a shallow sand pit. It took a massive onslaught of bullets down onto the refugees before the last two remaining warriors emerged from the hole and made a final charge against the ring of soldiers. The few women and children who had somehow escaped death in the pit were taken back to Fort Robinson.

Dull Knife, meanwhile, had managed to elude the troops by hiding in a cave. Starved, ill, and scantily clad in the sub-zero weather, he and the remnants of his family finally made it to the Sioux camps at the Pine Ridge agency of South Dakota. The surviving Cheyenne women and children were later sent there also, but seven Cheyenne men, including Chief Wild Hog, were taken to Kansas for trial. Largely for lack of witnesses to the Kansas depredations, the trial was never held. Instead, the seven and their families were returned to Darlington.

Little Wolf and his band remained in the Nebraska sand hills through the winter, living off the abundant antelope and deer. Troops scoured

the countryside for them without success. As spring approached, Little
Wolf moved up past the Black Hills in an effort to reach the Yellowstone
country and, perhaps, move on to Canada to join Sitting Bull. In late
March 1879, Little Wolf's band was intercepted on the Little Missouri
River in eastern Montana by a cavalry force under Lt. W. Philo Clark.
Little Wolf and his band surrendered peacefully.

Clark took them to Fort Keogh, where they and other Northern
Cheyenne warriors scouted and fought for General Miles in his campaigning against the Sioux and Nez Percé. With strong support from both
Miles and Clark, the government made no effort to return Little Wolf's
band to the Indian Territory.

More Indian fighting was ahead for the men involved in the
Cheyenne chase. In September 1879, Major Thornburgh led a combined
force of Third Cavalry, Fifth Cavalry, and Fourth Infantry south from Fort
Fred Steele, Wyoming, in an effort to rescue agent N. C. Meeker from his
Ute Indian charges in northern Colorado. Shortly after crossing the Milk
River, Thornburgh was killed by a Ute sniper.

General Miles had not given up on his hope of catching Sitting Bull
and kept his forces on patrol in Montana. Eventually hunger brought the
Sioux leader and his desperate band back onto U.S. ground in search of
food. During July 1879 a scouting detachment led by Lieutenant Clark discovered a party of Sioux men and women under Sitting Bull on the Milk
River. The Indians stoutly resisted, and it was only when Miles came forth
with two Hotchkiss cannon that the Sioux were finally driven back into
Canada. The Sioux dissident remained in exile for the next two years. But
with starvation driving many of his followers to defect to the Dakota
Indian agencies, he himself finally gave in, crossing the border with his
last 185 people to hand his rifle over to Miles at Fort Buford on July 19, 1881.

"I wish it to be remembered," he said defiantly, "that I was the last
man of my tribe to surrender my rifle."[1]

But though Sitting Bull had surrendered in body, he had not done so
in spirit. He remained unflinchingly opposed to any acceptance of white
influence. When the Ghost Dance movement swept the Sioux agencies in
1890, Sitting Bull embraced it as a way of contesting government control
over his people. He was ordered arrested. When troops surrounded his
cabin, Sioux warriors rushed to the rescue. In the bloody fight that
ensued, Sitting Bull was among those who were killed.

The death of the great Miniconjou leader ignited great passion
among the Sioux, and a new outbreak of warfare was feared. But it was

the peace efforts of Chief Big Foot that led to a great, final tragedy for the Sioux. In an attempt to calm the much-disturbed Oglalas, Big Foot led his Cheyenne River Miniconjous to the Pine Ridge reservation without securing the required approval of the U.S. Army. In making this unauthorized move, he aroused the fear and anger of General Miles, who issued orders that Big Foot be intercepted.

When units of the Seventh Cavalry found Big Foot on the White River, the old chief had become dangerously ill with pneumonia. He and his people willingly accepted escort to a camp on Wounded Knee Creek east of the Pine Ridge agency. There, on the bitterly cold morning of December 29, 1890, the Indians awoke to find themselves surrounded by some five hundred troops armed with four Hotchkiss artillery pieces. Col. James W. Forsyth demanded that the Indians turn over their arms. During a search of the lodges, the accidental misfiring of a rifle touched off an escalating melee of gunfire. When it was over, the field of carnage revealed 25 officers and men killed and over 150 Miniconjous dead, with many others on both sides wounded.

Among those killed was Big Foot. A battle site photograph was taken of his frozen body with fingers raised as if to speak, even in death, his wish to end the fighting. Few images could portray a more telling finale to the Indian Wars of the American Plains.

Books to Read

Brown, Dee. *Bury My Heart at Wounded Knee*. New York: Harcourt College Publishers, 1971; Reprint: New York: Henry Holt and Co., 2001.

Gonzales, Marie, and Elizabeth Cool-Lynn, eds. *The Politics of Hallowed Ground: Wounded Knee and the Struggle for Indian Sovereignty*. Urbana, IL: University of Illinois Press, 1998.

Hoig, Stan. *Perilous Pursuit, the U.S Cavalry and the Northern Cheyennes*. Boulder: University Press of Colorado, 2002.

Josephy, Alvin M., Jr. *The Nez Percé Indians and the Opening of the Northwest*. New Haven: Yale University Press, 1965.

Monnett, John H. *Tell Them We Are Going Home*. Norman: University of Oklahoma Press, 2001.

Powell, Father Peter. *People of the Sacred Mountain*. 2 vols. San Francisco: Harper & Row, 1981.

Sandoz, Mari. *Cheyenne Autumn*. New York: McGraw Hill Books, 1953.

Note

1. Robert M. Utley, *Frontier Regulars* (New York: Macmillan Publishing Co., 1973), 288.

PART
TWO

Visitor Site Guide

CHAPTER NINE

Texas Tour Guide

As a Spanish and then a Mexican province and later as an independent republic apart from Mexico or the United States, Texas engaged the tribes of the Southern Plains in a long and determined contest over control of its vast lands. Notable foes included the Lipan Apaches who ranged in southwestern Texas, New Mexico, and Mexico; the Comanches and Kiowas who emigrated south from the upper Rockies during the late 1700s; and a variety of smaller tribes such as the Tawakonis, Tonkawas, Anadarkos, Taovayas (a branch of the Wichitas at times known as Pawnee Picts), Wacos, Caddos, Kichais (or Keechis), and Plains (or Kiowa) Apaches. Collectively the Spanish knew them as *Norteños* (Indians of the North). Though there were periods under Spanish control when these tribes traded peacefully at San Antonio and other settlements, their war parties persistently raided haciendas in Texas and on beyond the Rio Grande into Mexico, taking captives and stock.

The constant increase in Texas's Anglo-American population brought a far more aggressive Indian resistance as well as military counterstrikes into the Indian-held prairie land of northern and western Texas. Peace was eventually achieved with the 1874 punitive campaign known as the Red River War. Forces under Gen. Nelson Miles attacked Kiowa, Comanche, Cheyenne, Arapaho, and Plains Apache camps in the Texas Panhandle and western Indian Territory. The starving tribes were eventually forced to capitulate and go to assigned reservations in Indian Territory.

Battle Sites

• **ADOBE WALLS, 1865 BATTLE OF:** Historical marker for the two Battles of Adobe Walls is located south off SH 281 between Stinnett and Spearman in

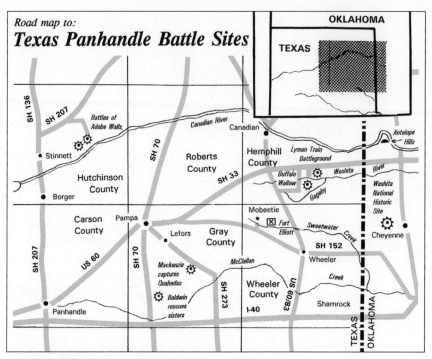

Texas Panhandle battle sites. (Courtesy of author)

northeast Hutchinson County. The site's six-acre tract is owned and managed by the Panhandle-Plains Historical Society. Though two important Indian engagements were fought here, the post was never a military fort. It was originally built as an Indian trading post by Bent and St. Vrain Co.

• **ADOBE WALLS, 1874 BATTLE OF:** Site location same as above.

• **BALDWIN'S VICTORY:** Historical marker for Baldwin's dramatic wagon attack on Grey Beard's camp is located ten miles southeast of Lefors on SH 273. Another marker, commemorating the rescue of the two Germain sisters from Grey Beard's camp, stands in a park at Lefors.

• **BUFFALO WALLOW FIGHT:** Granite monument for the Buffalo Wallow Fight is located fifteen and one-half miles southeast of Canadian, Texas, off US 60/83. Drive east on SH 277 seven miles to the dirt road, then south one mile to Monument. The River Valley Historical Museum, 118 N. Second St., features information and displays relating to the Lyman Wagon Train Siege and the Buffalo Wallow Fight with aerial views of the two sites. 806–323–6548.

- **ELM CREEK RAID:** Historical marker for the Elm Creek Raid is located on US 380 eight miles west of Newcastle. The granite marker commemorates the death of three 19-year-old boys who were killed on Elm Creek by Indians on July 17, 1867.
- **HOWARD WELLS FIGHT:** Site south of Fort Lancaster State Historical Park on I-10 is unmarked.
- **KICKING BIRD RAID:** Lieutenant McLellan's 1870 battle with the Kiowas under Kicking Bird is thought to have taken place six miles northwest of Archer City and south of Lake Kickapoo. Marker located in park on FM 25 two miles north of Archer City.
- **LYMAN WAGON TRAIN SIEGE:** Historical marker is located seven miles south on SH 60/83 from Canadian, Texas, and ten miles east on SH 33. The River Valley Historical Museum at Canadian features this battle site. See River Valley Historical Museum listing below.
- **NECHES RIVER BATTLE:** Historical marker commemorating the death of Chief Bowles is located near Redlands west of Tyler. The American Indian Cultural Society purchased sixty-eight acres around the battle site and erected a granite marker dedicated to the Cherokees who were killed there.
- **NORTH FORK BATTLE:** Site of Colonel Mackenzie's 1872 battle on the North Fork of the Red River is near SH 273 nine miles north from I-40 at McLean, Gray County, in the Texas Panhandle. Historical marker is located ten miles southeast of Lefors.
- **PALO DURO CANYON BATTLE:** Historical marker for Mackenzie's 1874 victory over the Indians is located five miles from the gate entrance on Park Rd. 5 in Palo Duro Canyon State Park, 800–792–1112. www.paloduro-canyon.com. See Panhandle-Plains Historical Museum at Canyon.
- **PARKER'S STOCKADE (FORT PARKER) MASSACRE:** This event is commemorated by the reconstructed post and visitor center in Fort Parker Historical Park off SH 1245, Park Rd. 35, north of Groesbeck. 254–729–5253.
- **PLUM CREEK BATTLE:** Historical marker is located on Plum Creek bridge in Lions' Park, Lockhart, near the intersection of US 183 and SH 142.
- **SAN SABA MISSION MASSACRE:** The Norteño massacre of San Saba Mission finds modern recognition in the partially restored ruins of its attendant fort, the Presidio San Luis de Las Amarillas at Menard. The historical marker located at the US 190 entrance to the site identifies the Arroyo de Juan Lorenzo (now Celery Creek) by which the Indians approached the mission undiscovered. Menardville Museum, SH 83 North. 915–396–2365

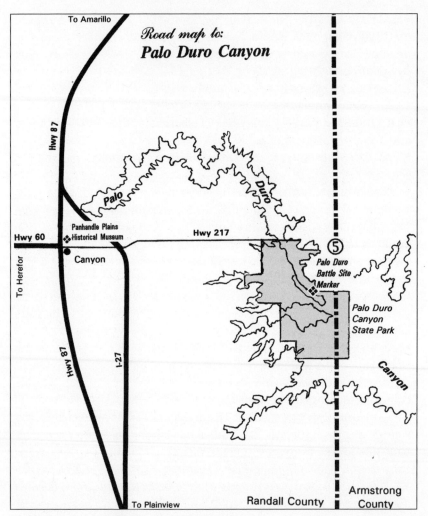

Palo Duro Canyon battle site. (Courtesy of author)

• **SPANISH FORT BATTLE:** Historical marker is located at Spanish Fort, Texas, on square across from old store on FM 103 some seventeen miles west of Nocoma. There were two Wichita villages: San Theodoro on the Texas side of the Red River and San Bernardo, located a mile and a quarter southwest of Petersburg on the Oklahoma side.

• **WARREN WAGON TRAIN MASSACRE:** Historical marker is located on SH 16 eight miles northeast of Graham.

Fort Sites

• **THE ALAMO**, Alamo Plaza, San Antonio: Though the Alamo stands today as the site of one of America's most famous battles—that between Texas revolutionists and Santa Anna's Mexican army in 1836—it also served at times as a headquarters for U.S. Army and Texas Ranger operations against the Indians. Visitors interested in exploring Texas Indian history can do so in the Texas State Library located on site. www.thealamo.org

• **FORT BELKNAP:** Located on SH 251 three miles southwest of Newcastle. Established in 1851 as the northern anchor of a second line of pre–Civil War forts extending from the Red River to the Rio Grande to monitor the Indian frontier of northern Texas. The fort also served as a Butterfield Overland Mail stop. Named for Lt. Col. William G. Belknap, Fifth U.S. Artillery, who selected its site. The post was surrendered to the Confederacy in 1861, then reoccupied by federal troops following the Civil War until 1867 when it was abandoned in favor of Fort Richardson. Some seventeen men who became Civil War generals served at the post, including Albert Sidney Johnston. He and his command marched from Missouri in 1855 during a terrible norther that froze the Brazos River over six inches deep, living in tents after their arrival. The site includes six original buildings and one replica building, recreational park, powder magazine, and picnic facilities. The two-story commissary building houses the museum. Tours are offered. An on-base historical marker notes the vital service of the Tonkawa scouts to the military in Texas. 940–846–3222. www.fortbelknap.org

• **BIRD'S FORT:** Marker one mile east of site on FM 157, one mile north of Trinity River in Arlington, the site of the post being nearby on private property. The stockade post was established during the winter of 1840–1841 by Capt. John Bird and his company of Texas Rangers to promote the initial settlement of the Dallas–Fort Worth region. A treaty conducted at the fort in 1843 attempted to draw a line between Texas and Indian territories. Indian trader Thomas Torrey died during the council.

• **FORT BLISS:** First established in 1849 and still active today, this much-moved fort has seen six locations within the present confines of El Paso. It is named for Capt. William Smith Bliss, Fourth U.S. Infantry, adjutant to Maj. Gen. Zachary Taylor during the Mexican War. Strategically located in regard to Mexican relations at the very southwestern tip of Texas, the post also guarded against Indian incursions. Kiowa tradition

Bird's Fort. (Courtesy of author)

tells of war party expeditions from the Indian Territory to the Hueco Tanks region just east of El Paso.

An adobe replica of the original post houses the Fort Bliss Museum and Study Center, Building 1735, Marshall Road; it offers exhibits and library facilities relating to the Indian wars and other historical aspects. 915–568–3390. www.bliss.army.mil/Museum

• **FORT CHADBOURNE NATIONAL HISTORIC LANDMARK:** Located eleven miles northeast of Bronte off US 277. A cemetery with tombstones dating back to the 1870s is nearby. Named for Second Lt. Theodore L. Chadbourne, Eighth U.S. Infantry, who was killed in the Mexican War. Established in 1852 to guard the frontier from Indian raiders, the fort also featured a Butterfield Overland Stage station. The fort was garrisoned by

Texas militia for a time during the Civil War and later reoccupied by federal troops. It was closed in favor of Fort Concho in 1868 because of inadequate water and wood. 915–743–2555. www.fortchadbourne.org

• **FORT CIBOLO (EL FORTIN DEL CIBOLO):** *Cibolo*, Spanish for buffalo. This private fort in Presidio County offered area citizens protection from Indian raids. The twenty-foot-high stockade walls of this one-story adobe were surrounded with broken bottles to hold off attackers. The post has been reconstructed as one-story adobe, cottonwood, and cypress structure with courtyard. Marker located five miles north of Shafter and then another four miles northwest on dirt road.

• **FORT CLARK:** This post was established near present Brackettville on June 24, 1852, and named for Maj. John B. Clark, First Infantry. Its purpose was to control the Mescalero and Lipan Apaches and Comanche Indians who raided along the Rio Grande. Originally a log stockade fort, it was upgraded with stone buildings during the 1850s. Federal troops departed at the outbreak of the Civil War, being replaced by the Second Texas Mounted Rifles. Col. Ranald Mackenzie led Seminole-Negro Indian scouts on raids into Mexico from Fort Clark. The fort was closed and sold for salvage in 1946. The Fort Clark Historical Society maintains the site as a Historic District with a museum and Seminole Indian Scouts' Cemetery, 3.1 miles south of Brackettville on FM 3348.

• **FORT CONCHO NATIONAL HISTORIC LANDMARK:** Located at San Angelo, this former cavalry post was established in 1867 to protect the vast West Texas frontier from Apaches and Indian Territory raiders. Originally named Camp Hatch, it was renamed for the Concho River in 1868. Fort Concho troops played a major role in the Red River War of 1874. Mackenzie's Quahada Comanche prisoners were housed there until their forced march of three hundred miles back to Fort Sill in the Indian Territory. Closed in June 1889, the well-preserved post still offers some twenty-three original and restored structures. The visitor center at Oakes and C Avenues provides information on military uniforms and weapons, artifacts, and living history programs such as The Fort Concho Buffalo Soldier. 915–481–2646, 915–657–4444. www.fortconcho.com

• **CAMP COOPER:** Marker located on RR 2528 off US 283, eight miles south and seven west of Throckmorton. Named for Col. Samuel Cooper, adjutant general of the U.S. Army. Robert E. Lee was stationed at the post for nineteen months during 1856–1857. It was never reopened after being surrendered to the Confederacy on February 21, 1861.

• **FORT CROGHAN:** Located at Burnet on the banks of Hamilton Creek. Named for Col. George Croghan, a hero in the 1812 Battle of Fort Stephenson. Originally a Texas Ranger station under Henry E. McCulloch, it was established in March 1849 as a forward defense post of that day and garrisoned by the Second U.S. Dragoons until closed in 1853. Its history is told at the Post Museum, 703 Buchanan Drive (SH 29, West), Burnet, where a blacksmith's shop, one-room schoolhouse, powder house, and stagecoach stop are featured along with numerous historic artifacts. 512–756–8281. www.fortcroghan.org

• **FORT DAVIS NATIONAL HISTORIC SITE:** Located at the intersection of SH 17 and 118, the original post was established in October 1854 as a counter to incursions by the Comanches, Kiowas, and Apaches. Named for Jefferson Davis, then the U.S. Secretary of War. During the Civil War, it was occupied at times by Confederate forces and at other times by renegade Indians and Mexicans. In September 1862, it was reclaimed for the Union by a unit of the First California Cavalry and reoccupied in 1867 by the U.S. Ninth Cavalry under Lt. Col. Wesley Merritt, who had the post rebuilt. It remained active until June 1891. Located among the Davis Mountains, the area was once popular as a resort. The 460-acre historic site, which was dedicated in April 1966, includes the Overland Trail Museum. 433–436–3224, ext. 26. www.fortdavis.com

In addition to a visitor center/museum and auditorium, located near the town of Fort Davis, the site features over twenty-five restored buildings and various ruins that comprised the original Indian-fighting fort of the 1880s. The museum displays numerous artifacts of the Indian wars. All of the African-American units established after the Civil War were stationed at the fort and served in protecting transportation routes and monitoring the Great Comanche and Mescalero Apache war trails. Special programs and tours are provided.

• **FORT ELLIOTT:** Established in February 1875 near the town of Mobeetie following the Red River War. The only remaining evidence of this Panhandle fort is the fifty-foot flagpole. Constructed from two large cedars hauled in from a canyon and lashed together, the pole now stands at Mobeetie. Named for Maj. Joel Elliott, who was killed at the Washita in 1868, Fort Elliott was finally abandoned in October 1890 and its buildings sold at auction. A roadside marker is located less than a mile west of the SH 152 and FM 48 intersection.

• **FORT EWELL:** Established in 1852 on the south bank of the Nueces River in La Salle County and named for Mexican War veteran Capt. Richard S.

Ewell. The poorly situated and poorly constructed post saw outbreaks of scurvy among troops stationed there before its closure in 1854. The site of the post is now abandoned.

• **FORT GATES:** Located six miles southeast of Gatesville on SH 36 at the town of Fort Gates. Named for Capt. Collinson R. Gates, Eighth U.S. Infantry, who served in the Mexican War. The fort was established in October 1849 on the Leon River and closed in March 1852 as settlements moved farther west.

• **FORT GRAHAM:** Site of fort northwest of Hillsboro is now covered by Lake Whitney. Probably named for Col. William H. Graham, Eleventh U.S. Infantry, who was killed in the Mexican War. The post was established in March 1849 and closed in October 1853. When Lake Whitney was built some of the rocks of its buildings were used in reconstruction of one-room fort structures at the lake. Cemetery marker is located four and one half miles north of Whitney on FM 933.

• **FORT GRIFFIN STATE HISTORICAL PARK:** Located on US 283 between Throckmorton and Albany, the park includes restoration of several original fort buildings and ruins of others. Named for Col. Charles Griffin, Thirty-fifth U.S. Infantry, who commanded the Texas military department. Constructed in 1867 by Sixth U.S. Cavalry troops under Col. Samuel D. Sturgis and closed in 1881, the garrison took part in the Indian wars of the time. The 505-acre park with fifteen hundred feet of riverfront features a herd of Texas longhorn cattle. The site also offers camping, sport, picnic, and restroom facilities as well as historical reenactments. Some of Texas's Longhorn cattle herd range at Fort Griffin. 800–792–1112. www.tpwd.state.tx.us/park/fortgrif

• **FORT HANCOCK:** Established in June 1882 to counter war parties from the Indian Territory and Mexican bandits from across the Rio Grande. First called Camp Rice, in May 1886 it was renamed for Gen. Winfield Scott Hancock, who had died three months earlier. Marker is 52 miles southeast of El Paso on US 80.

• **FORT LANCASTER:** Ruins on Live Oak Creek, ten miles northeast of Sheffield, on US 290. Established in 1855 to guard the San Antonio-El Paso road from Indian attacks, it was evacuated by the Union at the outbreak of the Civil War in 1861 and not reoccupied. The Fort Lancaster State Historical Park and Museum is located at Sheffield.

• **FORT MCINTOSH:** Founded on the Rio Grande near Laredo in November 1846 with the arrival of Capt. Mirabeau B. Lamar and the Laredo Guard of the Texas Volunteers. First called Camp Crawford after the U.S. Secretary of War, it was renamed in tribute to Lt. Col. James S. McIntosh, who was killed during the Mexican War. The post was a key link in the chain of forts along the Rio Grande, guarding against Comanche and Lipan Apache incursions. Complaining of police brutality, Black troops of the Twenty-fifth Infantry at McIntosh rioted in 1899, resulting in their transfer to Fort Reno, Oklahoma, and their eventual dismissal from the service by President Teddy Roosevelt. In 1946 the now-obsolete post was closed and its property divided among the U.S. Boundary Commission, City of Laredo, and Laredo Junior College.

• **FORT MCKAVETT STATE HISTORICAL PARK:** Located west of Menard on SH 864 at Fort McKavett, the fort was established in March 1852 atop a high bank of the San Saba River, for which it was first named, but was later renamed for Capt. Henry McKavett, Eighth U.S. Infantry. It was abandoned in the spring of 1859 when its troops were transferred to Camp Cooper. Federal troops under Col. Ranald S. Mackenzie reoccupied the post in 1868.

McKavett offers a wide variety of forty restored buildings and ruins whose stone walls are still standing. These include its schoolhouse, officer quarters, post headquarters, bakery, barracks, morgue, and hospital, which now serves as a visitor center. 915–396–2358.

• **FORT MASON:** Located at the town of Mason. Founded in 1851, the post operated as a second line of frontier outposts, and serving there were several men who would become Confederate generals, among them Robert E. Lee (who spent his final year here before joining the Confederacy), Albert S. Johnston, Earl Van Dorn, and E. Kirby Smith. Named for Second Lt. George T. Mason, Second U.S. Dragoons, who was killed in an Indian skirmish. After being occupied by Rebel troops for a time during the war, it was reactivated by the U.S. Fourth Cavalry in January 1867. A historical marker to the north on US 190 east of Brady records an 1866 Indian-settler conflict. The post was closed permanently in March 1869. Today the reconstructed officers' quarters stands on Post Hill overlooking the foundations of other structures. The Mason County Museum, 300 Moody St., Mason, housed in a schoolhouse built in the 1870s, displays memorabilia among other historical items from the old fort. 915–347–6242.

• **FORT PHANTOM HILL:** Located off SH 351 between Albany and Abilene. Its name is thought to be related to the surrounding countryside. Established in 1851 on the Clear Fork of the Brazos, this colorful and very photogenic fort served as a stage stop on the Butterfield Overland Mail route until 1861. Its early wooden structures burned after the fort was abandoned in 1854. Today only the remains of the post's chimneys and two stone buildings, surrounded by huge cactus clumps, stand as phantom-like reminders of its Indian-frontier past. Fort Phantom Foundation: 915–677–1309. www.fortphantom.org

• **FORT QUITMAN:** This adobe-constructed post was established in September 1858 on the north bank of the Rio Grande below El Paso. Named for Maj. Gen. John Anthony Quitman, who died a short time earlier. The post was taken over briefly by Confederate troops during the Civil War and reoccupied by federal troops in 1862. It was abandoned in 1863, regarrisoned in 1868, and abandoned for good in 1877. Its ruins can be found off I-10 by SH 111 from Sierra Blanca.

• **FORT RICHARDSON STATE PARK:** Located at Jacksboro, the post was established as regimental headquarters for the Sixth Cavalry in 1868 as the northernmost outpost in the Western Defense Line of Texas. Named for Maj. Gen. Israel B. Richardson, who was killed during the Civil War. Ranald Mackenzie and his Fourth Cavalry regiment operated from the heavily garrisoned post at one time. General Sherman was at Fort Richardson at the time of the nearby Wagon Train massacre in May 1871. The ensuing trial for Satanta and Big Tree was held at Jacksboro. Seven of the fort's original buildings have been restored, including the picket-style officers' quarters. The post remained active until 1878, and today the site offers modern camping and recreation facilities.

In addition to the restored officers' quarters, the park features a powder magazine, morgue, bakery, and commissary, plus campsites with electricity, restrooms, showers, hiking trails, and fishing pond. A museum is located in the former enlisted men's barracks. An interpretive center provides a history of the fort. 940–567–3506. For camping reservations: 512–389–8900.

• **FORT STOCKTON HISTORIC SITE:** Located in City of Fort Stockton on I-10. Originally established in March 1859 to protect the San Antonio–El Paso stage line from Indians. Named for Commodore Robert H. Stockton, U.S. Navy. The early name of its location—Comanche Springs on Comanche Creek—gives testimony to its Indian background. The adobe fort was burned by Confederate forces during the war and rebuilt by the Ninth U.S. Cavalry troops under Col. Edward Hatch when it was reoccupied in 1867. It was finally abandoned in 1886. The Anna Riggs Museum, 301 S. Main St., is housed in an old hotel that was once a stage stop. Recreation park, Fort Cemetery, tours, brochure. 915–336–2400.

• **FORT TERRETT:** Located two miles north of I-10 thirty miles east of Sonora. Named for First Lt. John C. Terrett, First U.S. Infantry, who was killed during the Mexican War. This post of brief existence was established in February 1852 to protect the frontier from Indian incursions between Forts Clark and McKavett. Because it was not on a military road, it was closed in late 1854. Some of the original stone buildings are still in use by the site's private owners.

• **FORT WORTH:** Nothing remains today of the original fort that was established on the Trinity River in January 1849 and later moved to the mouth of the Clear Fork. Named for Col. William Worth, Eighth U.S. Infantry, department commander who had died a month earlier, the post was abandoned in 1853 in deference to Fort Belknap, and settlers took possession.

• **PRESIDIO SAN LUIS DE LAS AMARILLAS:** Located on US 90 one and a half miles west of Menard. Established on May 4, 1757, to protect the Franciscan mission of Santa Cruz de San Sabá and guard over the region which was thought to contain silver mines. Original wooden structures of the presidio were replaced by stone buildings in 1761. Though in ruins, some of the mission's walls still stand much as they were when the Norteños attacked in 1758. An ancient Spanish aqueduct still functions at the site. The Menard County Museum, located in the old depot on US 83 North, provides information on the region's 250 years of history.

Other Sites to See

• **POSSUM KINGDOM STATE PARK:** Scenic 1,615-acre lake and park recreation area south of Graham.

• **CAMP SAN SABA:** Texas Ranger Camp, located eleven miles south of Brady on US 87/377.

Related Museums

• **AMARILLO:** Amarillo Museum of Art, 2200 S. Van Buren St. provides six galleries that are programmed with sixteen exhibitions per year, including the art of American and European masters. 806–371–5050. www.amarilloart.org

• **BORGER:** Hutchinson County Museum, 612 N. Main, tells the story of Coronado's conquistadors who marched across the Texas and Oklahoma Panhandles in 1541 and first encountered the Plains Indians of that region and Kansas. In addition to exhibits of Panhandle history, the museum houses Indian war artifacts and scale models of Adobe Walls. 806–273–0130. www.hutchinsoncountymuseum.org

• **CANYON:** The Panhandle-Plains Historical Museum is located on the campus of West Texas State A&M University at 2401 Fourth Ave. This museum, billed as the largest in Texas, offers an extensive gun collection, prehistoric fossils, a reconstructed pioneer town, a gallery of southwestern art, and other exhibits relating to the early history of the Texas Panhandle region. 806–656–2244. www.panhandleplains.org

• **CLARENDON:** Saint's Roost Museum, 610 E. Harrington St., features an exhibit of Indian artifacts. 806–874–2546.

• **CLAUDE:** Armstrong County Museum, 120 N. Trice St., is a six-building complex that includes a theater where historical productions are presented annually. One program deals with Panhandle pioneer cattleman Charles Goodnight. 806–226–2187.

• **CROSBYTON:** Crosby County Pioneer Memorial Museum, 101 W. Main St., features the Wayne J. Parker Collection of Native American artifacts along with a Llano Estacado mural, a diorama of Blanco Canyon, and twenty-three thousand pieces of Native American material that address the story of how early natives of the Llano Estacado region lived. The museum also features the period of the Texas pioneer farmer and rancher. 806–675–2331. www.crosbycountymuseum.com

• **EL PASO:** El Paso Museum of History, 2 Civic Center Plaza, is dedicated to understanding the significance of the U.S.-Mexican border's rich multicultural history. 915–858–1928.

• **FORT WORTH:** Amon Carter Museum, 3501 Camp Bowie Blvd., features one of the nation's foremost collections of Western art, featuring works by Frederic Remington, Charlie Russell, and many others. 817–738–1933. www.cartermuseum.org

HOUSTON: Buffalo Soldiers National Museum, 1814 Southmore, is dedicated to preserving the legacy and honor of the African-American soldier. Featured are regimental and individual histories, cavalry and infantry associations, photo gallery, and memorabilia of the frontier's Afro-American "Buffalo Soldier." 713–942–8920. www.buffalosoldiermuseum.com

• **JACKSBORO:** Jack County Museum, 23 W. Belknap, depicts period home life. 940–567–5410.

• **LIPSCOMB:** Wolf Creek Heritage Museum, 300 Main Ave., exhibits display on Red River War by schedule. 806–653–2131.

• **MOBEETIE:** Mobeetie Jail Museum, 0.8 mile south from SH 152-FM 48 intersection, offers Red River War exhibit on second floor relating to history of Fort Elliott. 806–845–2028.

• **PAMPA:** Freedom Museum USA, 600 N. Hobart St. and 101 Memorial Park Drive, displays guns, swords, uniforms, and other memorabilia of U.S. military history. 806–669–6066. www.freedommuseumusa.org

• **PAMPA:** White Deer Land Museum, 116 S. Culyer St., features exhibits relating to Baldwin's victory and rescue of the Germain sisters. 806–669–8041.

• **PANHANDLE:** Carson County Square House Museum, SW 207 and Fifth St., features information, artifacts, and exhibits on Red River War. 806–537–3524. www.squarehousemuseum.org

• **PLAINVIEW:** Museum of Llano Estacado, Mabee Regional Heritage Center, 1900 W. Eighth, includes tools, homes, and weapons of ancient Indian tribes among other historical artifacts of Texas Panhandle region. 806–296–4735.

• **TULIA:** Swisher County Archives and Museum, Memorial Bldg., 127 SW Second St., features exhibits and paintings of Mackenzie's Palo Duro victory. 806–995–2819.

• **WACO:** Texas Ranger Hall of Fame and Museum, I-35 at University Park Drive in Fort Fisher Park. The hall honors twenty-six Texas Rangers, the original ten having been selected by Stephen F. Austin in 1823. Contains books, photographs, artifacts, and oral histories of the Rangers. 254–750–8631. www.texasranger.org

Trails to Explore

The State of Texas offers an appealing and well-marked Forts Trail through its regions of Indian Wars. One trail makes a circuit, which can be intercepted at any point, from Fort Richardson at Jacksboro south to Fort Mason at Mason. The western route through Abilene and San Angelo takes a visitor to a bounty of important Indian-fighting forts: Fort Richardson at Jacksboro, Fort Belknap at Newcastle, Fort Griffin north of Albany, Fort Phantom Hill near Abilene, Fort Chadbourne at Bronte, Fort Concho at San Angelo, Fort McKavett near Menard, Fort Mason at Mason, and Fort Croghan at Burnet.

Rather than follow the circuit back north on an easterly route that, though filled with interesting historical features, contains no frontier forts, some travelers may wish to swing on west to Fort Parker at Groesbeck. This could take them past Fort Croghan at Burnet and the Texas Ranger Hall of Fame at Waco. Or, if desired, a traveler could head on west where Fort Terrett, Fort Lancaster, Fort Stockton, Fort Davis, Fort Quitman, Fort Hancock, and Fort Bliss offer further historical adventure.

The Archeological Division of the Texas Historical Commission has recently surveyed the several battle sites of the Red River War of 1874 in the Texas Panhandle. While some of these sites are on private land and unavailable to entry, the region offers an abundance of viewable historical lore. For additional information and brochure, call 512–463–6096. www.thc.state.tx.us

The streams of the Texas Panhandle high plains—the Canadian, Washita, and several branches of the Red River—drain southeastward toward the Gulf of Mexico. Once a grazing land of the buffalo, its short-grassed prairies are gashed severely in places by red-earth canyons and studded with stratified buttes, principally along the Canadian River. Its principal geological feature is the Palo Duro Canyon at Canyon. A serpentine line of cap rock runs north-south from the Canadian River to beyond the Red River elevating the Staked Plains westward into New Mexico.

The many sites of interest in the Texas Panhandle are spread over a wide area, though several of the principal battle sites are located within three adjoining counties. In Hutchinson County there are the sites of the two battles of Adobe Walls; in Gray County, Baldwin's attack on Grey Beard and Mackenzie's capture of the Quahadas; and in Hemphill County, the Buffalo Wallow fight, the Lyman Wagon Train siege, and Price's engagement (unmarked). Wheeler County contains the Fort Elliott/Mobeetie site. Miles's first engagement occurred in Armstrong County, and Mackenzie's Palo Duro victory took place in Randall County.

Those touring the region will likely wish to choose their own route. The following plan attempts to cover as many of the sites as possible in a continuous circuit, allowing for side trips as desired. Though the circuit can be intercepted at any point, a visit to Canyon and the Palo Duro Canyon makes a good starting point. There a person interested in the Red River War can visit the Palo Duro Canyon and the Palo Duro State Park. The historical marker for Mackenzie's victory over the Indians is located five miles from the gate entrance on Park Rd. 5. The Panhandle-Plains Historical Museum in Canyon and the Armstrong County Museum at Claude both feature artifacts and information regarding the Red River War as well as other historical matters.

Interstate 27 leads on north to Amarillo and US 60 to Panhandle (Carson County Square House Historical Museum), then north on SH 207 to Borger (Hutchinson County Museum) and Stinnett (Adobe Walls site and marker), back from Borger on SH 152 to Pampa (White Deer

Land Museum and Baldwin fight marker), SH 273 to Lefors (Baldwin fight marker and Mackenzie's capture of Quahada village marker), by choice of route to Mobeetie (Mobeetie and Fort Elliott historical markers), and SH 83 to Canadian (Buffalo Wallow Battle Ground marker, Lyman's Wagon Train Battle marker, Old Military Road marker, River Valley Pioneer Museum).

At this point the traveler can take SH 33 to the Washita Battlefield National Historic Site at Cheyenne, Oklahoma, where Custer attacked Black Kettle's Cheyenne camp in November 1868. The historic Antelope Hills, known to early travelers as the Boundary Mounds, stand nearby.

CHAPTER TEN

Oklahoma Tour Guide

In 1815 the U.S. Congress selected areas in the unsettled lands beyond the Mississippi River to which tribes of the East and South could be removed. Ultimately a region identified as Indian Territory came to include most of present Oklahoma except the Panhandle area. During the mid-1830s, tribes of the South and East were relocated in the hilly woodlands of eastern Indian Territory. They were separated from the tribes of the western prairie land by a growth of brush, scrub oak, and blackjack known as the Cross Timbers. This natural barrier, which stretched southward across the center of the territory and well into Texas, provided a division between the more domesticated eastern tribes and those of the Plains. Capt. Jesse Bean, accompanied by the noted author Washington Irving, explored as far west as the Cross Timbers in 1832. Irving provided an excellent descriptive account of this early exploration of present Oklahoma in his *Tour of the Prairies* (London: John Murray, 1835).

Conflicts between the eastern and western tribes quickly developed. The Plains Indians resented the intrusion of hunting parties from the emigrant tribes, while the latter suffered from raids on their livestock by war parties from the west. In an effort to resolve these conflicts as well as to monitor the emigrant tribes in their new locations, the United States established Fort Gibson on the Neosho River of northeastern Indian Territory and Fort Towson on the Red River during 1824. These posts also served as bases from which military parties explored out into the scantily known country of Indian Territory and made first contact with the Plains Indians.

The Wichita Indians were the first of the tribes known to inhabit the Plains between the Arkansas and Red Rivers. Originally encountered by

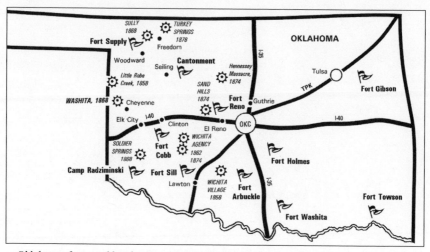

Oklahoma forts and battle sites. (Courtesy of author)

the Spanish in Kansas, the Wichitas were driven south by the Osages. The Comanches arrived on the Southern Plains during the late eighteenth century, followed soon after by the Kiowas. The Apaches often came into the region from the south to hunt and procure salt at the Great Salt Plains in northern Indian Territory. The Osage, Kansa (Kaw), Pawnee, and other tribes from the regions that are now Missouri, Kansas, and Nebraska constantly raided the rich horse herds of the resident Indians. Both this and hunting intrusions of the emigrant tribes resulted in numerous intertribal conflicts with the Plains tribes.

Battle Sites

• **HENNESSEY MASSACRE SITE:** Historical marker for Hennessey's grave is located on US 81 two blocks east of the Hennessey Memorial Garden.
• **LITTLE ROBE CREEK BATTLE:** No historical marker exists for this Texas Ranger battle, which occurred on private land northwest of the Antelope Hills off county road NS 172 in Ellis County, Oklahoma, west and south of present Arnett.
• **TURKEY SPRINGS BATTLE:** Precise site is still in question, but historical marker on US 64 north of Freedom denotes the general vicinity. Fenced burial site of Comanche Pool Cattle Co. salt haulers, who were killed by Cheyenne Indians during their flight, is on county line dirt road eleven miles due north of Freedom.

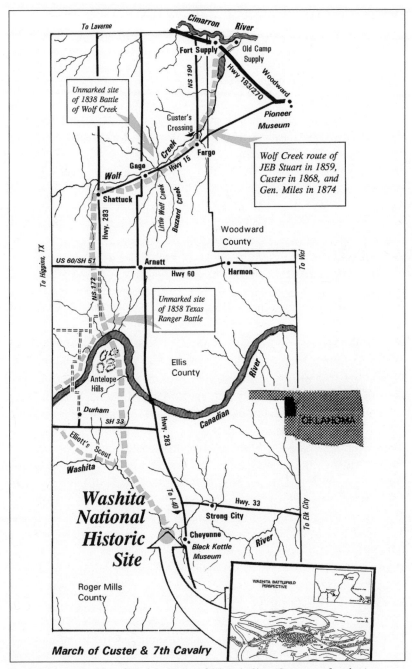

Battlefield perspective of Washita National Historic Site. (Courtesy of author)

• **WASHITA BATTLEFIELD NATIONAL HISTORIC SITE:** Located just west of Cheyenne off US 283, the battle site was recently made the ward of the U.S. National Park Service. Featured are a walking path, covered overlook, and historical marker. The site is a part of the Black Kettle and McClellan National Grasslands. The Black Kettle Museum in Cheyenne displays memorabilia relating to the Cheyennes and Custer's attack of November 27, 1868, on Black Kettle's village in which the famous chief was killed. The surprise, dawn attack was Custer's sole victory of note against the Indians. 580–497–3929. http://washitabattlefield.areaparks.com

•**WICHITA AGENCY BATTLE OF 1874** between U.S. troops and Kiowas: Historical marker for original agency is on US 62 eight miles west of Anadarko, Oklahoma, with agency grounds some five and a half miles north of historical marker. Following the 1862 attack, the agency was closed and reestablished after the Civil War at Anadarko.

• **WICHITA AGENCY MASSACRE OF 1862:** Site as noted above.

• **WICHITA VILLAGE BATTLE:** Historical marker for Van Dorn's 1858 attack is located at junction of SH 17 and US 81 at Rush Springs, Oklahoma.

Fort Sites

• **CANTONMENT:** Site of former Cantonment military base established in 1879 by Col. Richard I. Dodge is located at Canton, Oklahoma. A Mennonite Indian Mission was once situated here. Site features the Canton Area Museum and Canton Lake. Indian Mission School building has been reconstructed, but nothing of the old Cantonment remains, it having been dismantled in 1882. Canton Area Museum is located one block west of SH 51/SH 58 junction. 580–886–2266.

• **FORT ARBUCKLE, NEW:** Site located on SH 7 east of I-35 and Davis, Oklahoma, on Wild Horse Creek. Named for Col. Matthew Arbuckle, Seventh U.S. Infantry, who commanded at Fort Gibson for several years. The fort was established in 1851 to control Plains Indians of region. It was evacuated in May 1861 at the outbreak of Civil War and occupied by Texas Rebel troops, then burned by the Indians after the war. Union troops were stationed at the fort in 1866 and remained until it was closed in 1870. Only footing outlines of structures still exist. The Post Cemetery is located on the fort grounds.

• **FORT COBB:** Historical marker is on SH 9 just east of Fort Cobb, Oklahoma. Only indistinct trenches of site remain some three-quarters of a mile east of marker located on SH 9 in Fort Cobb, Oklahoma. Named for Treasury Secretary Howell Cobb. The fort was established in 1859 to oversee the newly created Wichita Indian agency. It was occupied by Confederate troops during the Civil War. Union forces returned to Cobb in 1868 for annuity distribution. Sheridan and Custer led their army there following the Battle of the Washita, with Kiowa chiefs Satanta and Lone Wolf held in chains. The fort was abandoned during the spring of 1869.

• **FORT GIBSON NATIONAL HISTORIC SITE:** Site is located on US 62 at Fort Gibson, Oklahoma, near the historic Three Forks confluence of the Arkansas, Verdigris, and Grand (Neosho) Rivers. Established in April 1824 in what became the Cherokee Nation, Indian Territory, in 1838. Named for Col. George Gibson, Commissary General, U.S. Army. The fort was occupied intermittently until 1857 when the Cherokee Nation took control of its buildings. Prior to the Civil War, the Fort Gibson military often rode forth to deal with the Plains tribes. Confederate troops occupied the post during the Civil War until it was retaken by Indian-supported Union troops. Reoccupied in 1866 and finally abandoned by the army in 1890. Some of its old buildings are still in use, and others have been recreated. An on-site Post Museum traces the fort's history from the early Indian removals to the post–Civil War period. A powder magazine built in 1842 still remains. Fort Gibson National Cemetery, 1423 Cemetery Rd., one mile east on US 62, includes the graves of veterans of the War of 1812 and on, plus those of the Plains Indian Wars and western Oklahoma exploration. 918–478–4088. www.ok-history.mus.ok.us/mus-sites/masnum06.htm

• **FORT HOLMES/CAMP MASON:** Specific site of the fort established near Lexington, Oklahoma, in 1834 is unknown. Named for Lt. Theophilus H. Holmes, Seventh U.S. Infantry, who built the first blockhouse and soldier quarters there. When the site was visited in 1845 by an exploring party under Lt. James W. Abert, all that remained were three or four posts, two stone chimneys among blackened ruins, and some abandoned wagons that had been burned. The post was closed in 1839.

• **FORT NICHOLS:** Some ruins of the Oklahoma Panhandle fort can be seen a mile west and two and one half miles north of Wheeless. Possibly named for Lt. Charles P. Nichols, First California Cavalry. The fort was established by Kit Carson in 1865 to protect transportation on the Santa Fe Trail's Cimarron Cutoff from Indian raiding. It was occupied by troops for less than one year. Traces of the Santa Fe Trail can still be seen a mile south of the fort.

• **CAMP RADZIMINSKI:** Historical marker is located on US 183, one mile north of Mountain Park, Oklahoma. Established by Lawrence S. (Sul) Ross of Maj. Earl Van Dorn's command in 1858 and named for First Lt.

Charles Radziminski, U.S. Second Cavalry, who had recently died of tuberculosis. The base camp, first located on Otter Creek near present Tipton and later moved upstream, was surrounded by a picket fence, while soldiers were quartered in Sibley tents and river bank dugouts. In March 1859 it was again moved to near Mountain Park. No buildings were ever erected, and only a pile of stones remains of the temporary site. Van Dorn marched from the camp to attack the Wichita village in 1878 and the Comanche camp in Kansas in 1879.

• **FORT RENO:** Established on the North Canadian River just south of the Darlington agency in July 1875, Fort Reno joined Fort Sill and Fort Supply in overseeing the Indians of western Indian Territory. Named for Maj. Gen. Jesse Reno, who was killed by friendly fire during the Civil War. A highlight of its history was the fort's Fourth Cavalry pursuit of the Northern Cheyennes under Dull Knife and Little Wolf to the Platte River during their famous retreat of 1878. The post became a Remount Depot in 1908 and continued to train horses and mules for the mechanized armies of both World Wars and the Korean conflict. Today Fort Reno is located due west of El Reno, Oklahoma, and features a visitor center, several of its original buildings, and a graveyard where frontier notables such as frontier scout Ben Clark and his Cheyenne wife are buried, plus a section containing the graves of World War II German prisoners. The former Darlington Indian agency, located south across the North Canadian River from Fort Reno, is now the property of Redlands College. A graveyard containing remains of people associated with Darlington is located on the road off US 81 leading to the Cheyenne and Arapaho Headquarters at Concho. Fort Reno Visitor Center: 405–262–3987. www.fortreno.org

• **FORT SILL:** This post features many original buildings, a visitor center/museum/library, and two Indian burial grounds. Located west of US 281 and the H. E. Bailey Turnpike three miles north of Lawton, Oklahoma, it was established in 1869 by General Sheridan to control the warring Cheyennes, Kiowas, and Comanches. The post was first garrisoned by Custer and the Seventh Cavalry and then by Tenth Cavalry Buffalo Soldiers under Col. B. H. Grierson. It is active today as a major field artillery training post. Of special interest are its Indian cemeteries in which are buried many noted Indian leaders such as Quanah Parker; his captive mother, Cynthia Ann; Delaware frontiersman Black Beaver; Kiowa chiefs Satanta, Satank, and Kicking Bird; and the renowned Apache leader Geronimo. The Sherman House, on the porch of which

General Sherman confronted Satanta, is featured. The house was built by Buffalo Soldiers of the Tenth Cavalry. The Fort Sill Museum occupies a building on the original post parade grounds. In addition to its library, the visitor center/museum holds historical documents and photos. 580–442–5123. http://sill-www.army.mil/Museum

• **FORT SUPPLY:** Located on US 270/412 near the town of Fort Supply. Thought also to be near the site of Thomas James's trading post of 1821. First established on November 18, 1868, as Camp Supply by Gen. Alfred Sully, who had earlier fought the Cheyennes inconclusively in the sand hills nearby. Custer and the Seventh Cavalry marched from here to do battle on the Washita. The post was enlarged and redesignated as Fort Supply following the Northern Cheyenne retreat of 1879. Cavalry, infantry, and Cheyenne scouts were garrisoned there. Today the site features a historic recreation of the stockade post near its original site, a visitor center, and a historic post cemetery. Fort Supply was abandoned as an active fort in 1893 and served for a time as a state hospital. A marker at the entrance of the cemetery notes the nearby archeological discovery in a bison-kill site of the oldest (ca. 10,500 years ago) ceremonial-painted buffalo skull in North America. Fort Supply Cavalry Day celebrations are held mid-September. 580–766–3767.

• **FORT TOWSON:** This reconstructed stockade military post is located one-half mile east and one mile north of Doaksville. Founded in 1824 by Maj. Alexander Cummings, Seventh Infantry, this fort monitored the relocation of the Choctaw Indians, dealing with problems of both the Choctaws and resident whites along the Red River resulting from Plains Indian depredations. It also played a prominent role in the movement of troops during the Mexican War. Named for Col. Nathan Towson, paymaster general of the U.S. Army. The post was abandoned in 1854. Visitor Center: 580–873–9385.

• **FORT WASHITA:** Site is located on SH 199, eleven miles east of Madill. Established by Zachary Taylor in April 1842 to protect Chickasaw Indians from Plains Indian raiders. It was abandoned by Union forces in 1861 and occupied by Confederate troops until destroyed by fire in 1865. Some original structures still exist, and some restoration has been done. The site offers a picnic area and restrooms. Visitor Center: 580–924–6502.

Other Sites to See

• **ANTELOPE HILLS:** Located north from Durham on dirt road. In November 1868, Custer and his staff surveyed the snow-covered landscape from atop one of the bluffs on their way to the Washita. Originally called Boundary Mounds, the bluffs were a valuable landmark on the Canadian River gold rush trail to California and the center of countless Indian buffalo hunts.

• **CUSTER RENDEZVOUS:** Historical marker on grounds of Quartz Mountain State Park, Kiowa County, notes point where Custer met a supply train and began his Texas Panhandle expedition of March 1869 in which he rescued two captive white women.

• **GLASS MOUNTAINS:** US 412 from Enid to Woodward passes through the ocher, mica-streaked buttes known as the Glass Mountains.

• **JESSE CHISHOLM GRAVE:** Drive north from Geary, and follow roadside markers east off US 270/281 to the grave marker of Jesse Chisholm, the noted Cherokee frontiersman and trader who was a friend and advisor to chiefs of the Plains tribes.

• **LEAVENWORTH EXPEDITION:** Camp Comanche marker on US 62 at line between Caddo and Comanche counties commemorates the initial visit of U.S. troops with the Comanche Indians near the Wichita Mountains in 1834.

• **LITTLE SAHARA SAND DUNE RECREATION AREA:** Unique sand dunes noted by early explorers are located south of Waynoka on US 281. Waynoka maintains a historical museum featuring Santa Fe railroad history.

• **QUANAH PARKER STAR HOUSE:** Home of famous Comanche chief, son of Cynthia Ann Parker, is located at Cache. 580–429–3238.

• **RED ROCK CANYON:** Located at Hinton. 405–542–3413.

• **ROCK MARY:** Historical marker for this prominent landmark on the California Road along the Canadian River is on US 281 a mile south of Hinton.

• **ROMAN NOSE STATE RESORT PARK:** Located eight miles north of Watonga, on SH 8 and SH 8A, this resort area was once the camping site for the Cheyenne Indians, U.S. Dragoons, buffalo hunters, U.S. Cavalry, outlaws, and U.S. marshals. It now features cabins, riding trails, golf, fishing, and Western reenactments. Lodge: 580–623–7281, 800–832–8690.

• **SANTA FE TRAIL:** Historical marker on SH 25 fifteen miles west of Boise City indicates route of the famous trail across western tip of Oklahoma Panhandle. It was somewhere on this route that Western explorer Jedediah Smith was killed by unknown Indians.

• **SEGER COLONY:** The Cheyenne and Arapaho school at Colony was begun in 1866 by John H. Seger, well known for his work among the Plains Indians.

• **WICHITA VILLAGE:** Historical marker at junction of US 283 and SH 44 for Wichita (Toyash) village visited by Col. Henry Dodge and painted (from sketch made by friend) by George Catlin.

Related Museums

• **ALTUS:** Museum of the Western Prairie, 1100 N. Memorial Dr., provides history of old Greer County and southwestern Oklahoma. 580–463–2441.

• **ANADARKO:** Delaware Tribal Museum, located two miles north of Anadarko on US 281, displays traditional clothing, beadwork, and artifacts of the Delaware tribe. The Delawares, originally situated in the East, were known for their roaming propensity. A number of their leading men, including the highly regarded Black Beaver, were noted Western scouts. 405–247–2448.

• **ANADARKO:** Indian City, USA, located near Anadarko two and a half miles southeast on SH 8, offers visitors tribal dancing, lectures, a museum, and authentically restored Indian dwellings. A restaurant and gift shop are available. 405–247–5661, 800–433–5661. www.indiancityusa.com

• **ANADARKO:** The National Hall of Fame for Famous American Indians, located on the east side of town, features busts of Native Americans. 405–247–5555.

• **ANADARKO:** Southern Plains Indian Museum and Craft Center, 715 E. Central, provides exhibits and galleries devoted to the creative work of Native American artists. 405–247–6221.

• **CARNEGIE:** Kiowa Tribal Museum and Resource Center, a quarter mile west on SH 9, displays murals by Kiowa artists interpreting Kiowa heritage. 580–654–2300.

• **CLINTON:** Cheyenne Cultural Center located on west side of Clinton on US 66 features Indian art and crafts. Also in Clinton is Route 66 Museum, which replicates a highway stop of the thirties. 580–323–6224. www.route66.org

• **EL RENO:** Canadian County Historical Museum, located in the former Rock Island Depot at 300 S. Grand, specializes in Fort Reno and Rock Island Railroad history and includes a Buffalo Soldier exhibit. 405–262–5121.

• **ENID:** Museum of the Cherokee Strip, 507 S. Fourth, relates to the 1893 opening of the Cheyenne/Arapaho reservation, which was monitored by troops from Fort Reno and Fort Supply. Also in Enid is the Railroad Museum of Oklahoma containing a large collection of railroad memorabilia. 580–237–1907.

• **GOODWELL:** No Man's Land Museum, 207 W. Sewell at Panhandle State University, offers history of Oklahoma Panhandle region, including Indian artifact collections. 580–349–2670.

• **KINGFISHER:** Chisholm Trail Museum, 605 Zellers Ave., features Oklahoma Land Run of 1889 exhibits with pioneer schoolhouse, jail, plus Cheyenne/Arapaho historical artifacts and photos. Many Cheyenne and Arapaho descendants reside in Kingfisher. 405–375–5176.

• **LAWTON:** Museum of the Great Plains, 601 NW Ferris, offers cultural and natural history of the Southern Great Plains. Museum includes the Tingley Collection of Natural Artifacts, research library, and archives. 580–581–3460. www.museumgreatplains.org

• **OKLAHOMA CITY:** Oklahoma Historical Society, Wiley Post Building, 2100 N. Lincoln, Oklahoma Capital complex, features the State Museum of History, a library, archives, and a much-used Historical Research Center. A handsome new historical complex has opened its doors to the public. 405–521–2491. www.ok-history.mus.ok.us

• **OKLAHOMA CITY:** National Cowboy Hall of Fame and Western Heritage Center, 1700 NE Sixty-third St., offers superb Western art collections, including Russells, Remingtons, and many others; a 14,000-square-foot turn-of-the-century Western town; artifacts; and historical displays of the Old West. 405–478–2250. www.nationalcowboymuseum.org

• **PAWNEE:** Pawnee County Historical Society Museum, 513 Sixth St., focuses in part on the Pawnee Indians who were moved to Oklahoma during 1873 and 1874. 918–762–2108. www.pawneechs.org

• **PAWNEE:** Historic Indian Agency Monument, one-half mile east on Agency Road, honors Pawnee leaders of the past. 918–762–3621.

• **PAWNEE:** Pawnee Bill Ranch Historic Site and Museum, 1141 Pawnee Bill Rd., reflects the life and times of Wild West showman Gordon W. Lillie, "Pawnee Bill." 918–762–2513.

• **TULSA:** Gilcrease Museum, 1400 Gilcrease Museum Rd., offers one of the world's largest collections of American Western art, library and historical document collection, restaurant facilities, themed gardens. 918–596–2700. www.gilcrease.org

• **WOODWARD:** Plains Indians & Pioneers Museum, 2009 Williams Ave., focuses on Plains tribes, homesteading, ranching. The museum features an art gallery and gift shop. 580–256–6136. www.plainsindiansandpioneersmuseum.org

Trails to Explore

• **WOLF CREEK WAR ROAD:** To retrace Custer's 1868 march from the mouth of Wolf Creek to the Antelope Hills and on to the site of the Washita attack, a motorist can follow, in part, a route much used by other military commands and personages involved in Plains Indian warfare (see map, p. 123). In 1859 Lt. J. E. B. Stuart, Custer's Civil War foe, led a company of U.S. Dragoons up Wolf Creek in search of Indians. Van Dorn in 1859 and Sturgis in 1860 crossed near the Beaver–Wolf Creek juncture on their way north to do battle.

Custer's Crossing of Wolf Creek (unmarked) is located northwest of Fargo, and Custer took time to hunt buffalo in the snow south of Gage. Gen. Nelson Miles and his army of Sixth Cavalry and Fifth Infantry marched along the same route on his Red River War campaign of 1874, and scouts Billy Dixon and Amos Chapman, the latter with a wounded leg that would soon be amputated, retreated down Wolf Creek after their Buffalo Wallow fight. During the 1880s, cargoes of buffalo hides were hauled by ox train from the Texas Panhandle via Camp Supply to the Dodge City railhead. The trail later became the Fort Elliott–Fort Dodge military road. Site of 1838 Battle of Wolf Creek is unmarked.

Custer's route (see map of Custer's 1868 march, p. 123) can be followed fairly closely by taking US 270 north from Fort Supply three miles to NS 190 and following it southwestward along Wolf Creek to Fargo. Early accounts tell of Indian encampments along this stretch of Wolf Creek, and the 1838 Battle of Wolf Creek is thought to have occurred somewhere along the north bank of the creek here.

To continue on Custer's route, one can follow SH 15 west from Fargo to Shattuck and take US 283 south to US 60, where the Antelope Hills become visible. From Arnett one approach to the Antelope Hills can be had by turning east on US 60/SH 51 to US 283 and south to Cheyenne. A more adventurous route would be to follow US 60/SH 51 west six miles to SH 46 and turn south on NS 172 (a dirt road not shown on most road maps), then follow it south to the Canadian River bridge and on to Durham en route to Washita National Historic Site at Cheyenne. This road passes by the unmarked site of the 1858 Battle of Little Robe Creek.

At Durham turn south to SH 33, east to US 283, and south to Cheyenne and the Washita Battlefield National Historic Site. From Cheyenne, one can opt to drive southeast to other sites such as Fort Sill at Lawton or turn west on SH 47 to explore the Texas Panhandle sites.

CHAPTER ELEVEN

Kansas Tour Guide

K ansas held a mid-Nation position that brought it in contact with many of the tribes of the Central Plains. To the east were the Osage and Kaw, plus several Eastern tribes that had been forced west: the Pottawatomie, Delaware, Sac and Fox, Seneca, and New York Indians. To the north and east were the Sioux, Pawnee, Otto, Missouri, and Omaha tribes; on the south the Kiowas, Comanches, Plains Apaches, and Wichitas, these last being Kansas residents at the time of Coronado's visit in 1541 and Oñate's in 1601. Dominating its western buffalo regions were the affiliated Southern Arapahos and Southern Cheyennes, who had split away from bands to the north, and, quite often, bands of Lakota Sioux.

From Fort Leavenworth, established in 1827, military expeditions set forth to establish relations with the tribes and quell disturbances up the Missouri River as well as along two of America's most significant roads westward, the Santa Fe and Oregon Trails. These routes were magnets that drew conflict, as often perpetrated by whites as by Indians. There are accounts of numerous clashes along the two overland trails that have been essentially forgotten today and which bear no commemorative marker.

The forward thrust of Anglo-Americans made Kansas settlements prey to the grievances of tribesmen. Commissioners came to talk peace and make promises that were seldom kept. Further troubles followed, bringing frontier armies of the United States marching across Kansas. As a result, Kansas became a warring ground where the contest between Indian and white concerns was often fierce and cruel.

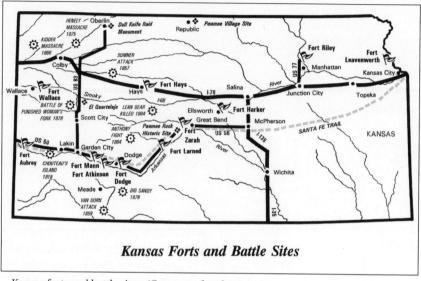

Kansas Forts and Battle Sites

Kansas forts and battle sites. (Courtesy of author)

Battle Sites

• **CHOUTEAU'S ISLAND BATTLE:** Historical marker on US 50 one mile west of Lakin.

• **COW CREEK STATION:** Marker on US 56 in Rice County tells of historic hand-dug well where Indians besieged Buffalo Bill Mathewson and wagon train in 1864.

• **HENELY MASSACRE:** Unmarked site located on private property twelve miles south on SH 25 and three miles east from Atwood, where Lt. Austin Henely and his men massacred a Cheyenne camp in 1875.

• **KIDDER MASSACRE:** Historical marker stands on the east side of gravel road SH 161 just south of Beaver Creek midway between Bird City and Edson in Sheridan County.

• **LINCOLN COUNTY MASSACRE:** Monument to the victims of Cheyenne raids against settlements along the Saline River in 1864, 1868, and 1869 stands at the courthouse square of Lincoln. Historical marker located two miles east of Lincoln on SH 18.

• **LONE TREE MASSACRE:** Historical marker for this massacre of six surveyors is located a mile and a quarter west of Meade on US 54/160. The name of site is taken from the lone cottonwood tree under which the surveyors were buried.

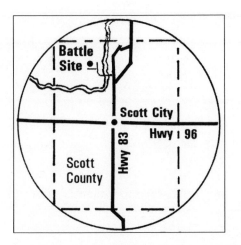

Road map to Punished Woman's
Fork battle site. (Courtesy
of author)

• **OBERLIN MEMORIAL:** Located in the Oberlin cemetery at the junction of US 36 and US 83, "The Last Indian Raid in Kansas" Monument
overlooks the graves of settlers who were killed by the Northern
Cheyennes in September 1878. Testimonies and accounts of other citizens involved in the raid are available in the Decatur County Museum
at Oberlin.

• **OSBORNE COUNTY:** Last Indian fight in Kansas, July 3, 1870. Marker
located on US 24 near Bloomington.

• **PUNISHED WOMAN'S FORK STATE PARK:** This significant battle site
north of Scott City on US 83 still maintains its natural setting, permitting
close access to and excellent visualization of the contest between a U.S.
Army command and the Northern Cheyenne Indians who sought to
entrap the pursuing troops in a canyon. Cheyenne rifle pits are identifi-
able along the canyon rim. The cave where the Cheyenne women and
children were secluded still exists. The Keystone Gallery Museum is
located in Scott City. Information and directions can be obtained at the
Ranger Station in the Park. www.keystonegallery.com

• **RAILROAD CREW MONUMENT:** Historical marker on E. Wichita Ave. and
Cindy Drive in Russell relates killing of two railroad workers by Indian
war party in May 1869.

• **ROMAN NOSE RAID:** Historical marker on US 40 east of Wallace tells of
raid in June 1867 by three hundred Cheyennes on overland stage station
and troops from Fort Wallace under Capt. Alfred Barnitz. Several soldiers
were killed.

• **SUMNER/CHEYENNE BATTLE** (see Chapter 3)**:** Historical marker located east of Hoxie on US 24.

• **VAN DORN ATTACK ON A COMANCHE VILLAGE:** Unmarked site on Crooked Creek in Meade County north of present Fowler.

• **WAGON BED SPRINGS:** Historical marker on US 270 eleven miles south of Ulysses indicates Cimarron River oasis on Santa Fe Trail where Indians frequently plundered wagon trains. Near there in 1831, the noted Western explorer Jedediah Smith was killed by Indians.

Fort Sites

• **FORT ATKINSON:** Site is located on north bank of the Arkansas River six to eight miles above Dodge City. Constructed in 1850 of adobe bricks and canvas roof to guard the Santa Fe Trail, it was garrisoned by a small force of infantry and First Dragoons. In July 1852 some ten thousand Indians who were gathered there to receive treaty annuities became severely agitated. A near war was averted by William Bent, who pacified the Indians until agent Thomas Fitzpatrick finally arrived with the promised annuity goods. Another near-conflict occurred the following year when an army officer angrily flogged a Cheyenne warrior whom he believed had acted improperly with another officer's wife. Nothing of the fort remains today.

• **FORT DODGE:** Established in 1864 as supply base of operations in Indian War. Located four miles southeast of Dodge City on US 400. Some of the post's old buildings are now a part of the Kansas Soldiers' Home, which includes a park and a library/museum. In nearby Dodge City, Boot Hill and the Beesom Museum commemorate the Santa Fe Trail, Texas cattle drives, and Wild West figures such as Wyatt Earp and Bat Masterson. 620–227–8188.

• **FORT HARKER:** Located a mile northeast of Kanopolis, the fort served largely as a supply base from 1864 until it was closed in 1873. Major General Hancock's command camped at Harker on its way to Pawnee Fork in 1866. When Elizabeth Custer saw it in 1866, it was "a forlorn little post—a few log houses bare of every comfort, and no trees to cast a shade on the low roofs."[1] Later, stone buildings were erected, and some of them still remain. The Fort Harker Museum is located in Kanopolis. 785–227–8188.

• **FORT HAYS:** Built in 1865 to protect Kansas-Pacific railroad workers and travelers on the Smoky Hill stage route to Colorado. Site is located in the Frontier Historical Park of Hays City, where a museum is maintained by the Kansas State Historical Society. Featured are a stone blockhouse, guard house, and two officers' quarters. 785–625–6812.

• **FORT LARNED NATIONAL HISTORIC SITE:** Fort Larned was established in 1859 as a distribution point for Indian annuities. The Fort Larned National Historic Site is located six miles west of Larned on SH 156. Named for Col. Benjamin F. Larned, army paymaster general. Now privately owned, the site offers recreational activities and historical instruction. The old military post on the Santa Fe Trail, the ruts of which are still visible nearby, is well restored and features a visitor center with a museum, library, and bookstore. The site also offers a nature trail. Santa Fe Trail Center Museum: 316–285–2054. www.larned.net/trailctr

• **FORT LEAVENWORTH NATIONAL HISTORIC SITE:** Located on US 73 just north of the town of Leavenworth; named for Col. Henry Leavenworth, Third U.S. Infantry. Established in 1827 to protect the Missouri fur trade as well as transportation on the Santa Fe and Oregon Trails, Leavenworth is the oldest active fort west of the Mississippi River. The Frontier Army Museum displays military uniforms of the day and information on a variety of famous military men—including George Custer (who was court-martialed there), Douglas MacArthur, and Dwight Eisenhower—all of whom were stationed at Fort Leavenworth. Tours: 913–684–3186. General information: 913–684–3191/3767. www.leavenworth.army.mil

• **FORT MANN:** Site is located some eight miles west of Dodge City. Built by and named for Capt. Daniel P. Mann, the fort was established during the spring of 1847 as a wagon repair and animal replacement depot. Though not an official military post, it was occupied on occasion by troops until it was abandoned in 1850 in favor of Fort Atkinson. Nothing visible of the fort remains.

• **FORT RILEY:** Located off I-70 north of Junction City. Named for Capt. Bennett Riley, First U.S. Infantry. Founded in 1853 to protect transportation on the westward trails, Fort Riley was "beautifully situated on a wide plateau, at the junction of the Republican and Smoky Hill river."[2] The parade ground square was surrounded by buildings a story and a half high, with the sutler's store, quartermaster and commissary storehouses, and cavalry stables to the outside. It was here that Custer helped transform the famous Seventh Cavalry Regiment to Indian warfare following the Civil War. For many years, the post featured the world's largest cavalry school and Cavalry Museum. Fort Riley remains an active military post today. 785–239–2737. www.riley.army.mil/Recreation/Museums

• **FORT WALLACE:** Located two miles from US 40, southeast of Wallace. Named for Brig. Gen. William H. L. Wallace, who was killed in the Battle of Shiloh. Established during 1865 deep in Indian-held country to protect the Smoky Hill stage route and Kansas-Pacific rail line, Wallace was much involved in the conflicts of western Kansas and eastern Colorado. In 1867, Mrs. Custer saw it as "almost as dreary as any spot on earth."[3] The fort prison was a hole in the ground, the prisoners being "locked up" by withdrawing the ladder. The post was abandoned in 1882, and its physical structures have disappeared; only the post cemetery remains. 785–891–3564.

• **FORT ZARAH:** Marker is on US 56 three miles east of Great Bend. Named by Maj. Gen. Samuel R. Curtis for his son Maj. Henry Zarah Curtis, who was killed by the Civil War bushwacker William C. Quantrill at Baxter's Spring. The fort was built to protect Santa Fe Trail transportation in 1864. Treaty talks were held with the Cheyennes at Zarah during 1866; an attack by Kiowas was repulsed there in October 1868. The fort was closed in 1869, and nothing of it remains visible.

Other Sites to See

• **CIMARRON (SANTA FE) CROSSING:** Though Santa Fe crossings of the Arkansas River varied, they occurred in the general area of Cimarron and Ingals. A marker in the park at Cimarron commemorates one such crossing.

• **EL QUARTELEJO PUEBLO NATIONAL HISTORIC SITE:** Located a short distance north of Scott City and Punished Woman's Fork. The settlement was first established during the sixteenth century by Indians fleeing from the New Mexico pueblos, it later becoming a trading center of the early Plains. The site's museum features a large collection of prehistoric fossils.

• **KANSA (KAW) INDIAN TREATY COUNCIL:** Marker on US 81 south of Elyria. Council conducted August 16, 1825.

• **LITTLE ARKANSAS TREATY COUNCIL SITE:** Marker on old US 81 one mile west of Park City. Treaty council featured famous names such as Kit Carson, William Bent, Jesse Leavenworth, William S. Harney, Black Kettle, Satanta, and others.

• **MEDICINE LODGE TREATY SITE:** Treaty grounds are located one mile east of Medicine Lodge off US 160. This grandiose council in October 1867 involved some fifteen thousand Cheyenne, Arapaho, Kiowa, Comanche, and Plains Apache Indians and five hundred soldiers. Attending were famous generals, frontiersmen, and Indian leaders of the

West. A number of national correspondents, including Henry M. Stanley who became famous as an African explorer, reported the event in great detail. Monument on city high school grounds.

• **PAWNEE INDIAN VILLAGE MUSEUM:** Eight miles north of US 36 on SH 66 in Republic. Site contains the evacuated lodge floor of an 1820's village where as many as two thousand Indians once lived. 785–361–2255.

• **PAWNEE ROCK:** Site is one-half mile northeast of the town of Pawnee Rock off US 56. Because it provided a lookout and place of ambush for Indians, it was once considered by some the most dangerous place on the Santa Fe Trail. While standing guard one night in 1826, young Kit Carson shot his mule, which he had mistaken for an Indian. Atop Pawnee Rock is a concrete shelter and interpretive plaque.

• **QUIVIRA:** Legendary site visited by Francisco Vasquez Coronado in 1851 and where Indians killed Franciscan friar Juan de Padilla the following year. Marker on US 56 between Lyons and Chase.

• **REBEL MASSACRE SITE:** An Indian battle that was not a part of the U.S. Indian Wars occurred in May 1863, during the Civil War, between a party of twenty Confederate officers and a band of loyal Osage Indians on the Verdigris River. The Rebels, led by gunman Charlie Harrison of Denver fame, were on their way from Carthage, Missouri, to Colorado Territory to recruit men and raid the lucrative gold and silver mine routes. The Osages killed and cut off the heads of all but two of the Confederates, who escaped along the river bank. A historical marker is located three miles north and one east of Independence on US 75.

Related Museums

• **ASHLAND:** Pioneer-Krier Museum contains collection of items from pioneer days as well as exhibits from the Clark County Fossil Beds.

• **COLBY:** Prairie Museum of Art and History, 1905 S. Franklin Ave., exhibits artifacts of early Kansas settlement, including period church, barn, sod house, windmill, and farm home. 785–460–4590. www.prairiemuseum.org

• **ELLSWORTH:** Hodgen House Museum Complex, 104 SW Main, displays a livery stable, one-room school, log cabin, general store, turn-of-the-century depot and caboose, and wooden windmill. 785–472–3059.

• **GARDEN CITY:** Finney County Museum, 403 S. Fourth, offers collections of artifacts, historical photos, and research material relating to southwest Kansas. Gift shop available. 620–272–3264, 800–879–9803.

• **HAYS:** Ellis County Museum, 100 W. Seventh, recreates features of 1880s day of Wild Bill Hickok and Buffalo Bill Cody with Western saloon, artifacts, historical photos, harness shop, and two Western murals. 785–625–6812. www.elliscountyhistoricalmuseum.org

• **KANOPOLIS:** Fort Harker Guardhouse Complex, 308 W. Ohio, offers post guardhouse, junior officer quarters, and a depot. 785–472–5733.

• **KINGMAN:** Kingman County Museum, 400 N. Main, two-story Renaissance building displays period tack room and horse equipment, stagecoach, furniture, medical equipment, fire trucks, and airplanes. 620–532–5274.

• **LAKIN:** Kearny County Museum, 111 S. Buffalo, features Santa Fe Trail displays, including a Conestoga wagon and restored Santa Fe Railroad depot. 620–335–7448. www.lakinkansas.org

• **MEADE:** Meade County Historical Society Museum, 200 E. Carthage, provides details on "Lone Tree Massacre" of surveyor party in 1874 that occurred near Meade. 316–873–2224. www.museumsusa.org/museums/info/1158609

• **NORTON:** Norton County Museum, 105 E. Lincoln, tells story of 1843 visit by Fremont expedition, the country as Plains Indian homeland, and pioneer days. Exhibits include meteors that have struck the area, prehistoric animal bones discovered locally, and the Norton County excavation of ancient Pawnee Indian site. 785–877–3313. http://nchistory.hosted.nextech.com

• **OBERLIN:** Last Indian Raid Museum, 258 S. Penn, holds documents, maps, and other information on the 1878 retreat of Northern Cheyennes through Kansas—"Last Indian Raid in Kansas." Gift shop available. 785–475–2712. http://www.skyways.org/museums/lirm

• **TOPEKA:** The Kansas History Center located off I-70, Exit 356, at 6425 SW Sixth St., Topeka, offers exhibits and information regarding the Kansas Plains Indian Wars in its museum, library, archives, and research center. 785–272–8681. www.kshs.org/places/khc

• **ULYSSES:** Historic Adobe Museum, 300 E. Oklahoma Ave., relates to the Cimarron Cutoff of the Santa Fe Trail. Historic Wagon Bed Springs is located ten miles south on SH 25. 203–356–3009. www.historicadobemuseum.org

• **WICHITA:** Old Cowtown Museum, addresses the settlement of Wichita and its early West aspects, featuring the historic story-and-a-half log Munger house. 316–778–2121. www.old-cowtown.org

• **WICHITA:** Wichita-Sedgwick County Museum, 204 S. Main, features historical aspects of early Wichita and surrounding region. 316–265–9314. www.wichitahistory.org

Trails to Explore

Both the historic Oregon and Santa Fe Trails through Kansas are well marked by the State. Today the Santa Fe scenic route from I-135 at McPherson offers a motorist the opportunity to follow US 56 and US 50 west past the sites of Fort Zarah, Pawnee Rock, Fort Larned, Fort Dodge, and Cimarron to Garden City. From there US 83 leads north to Scott City and the 1878 battle site of Punished Woman's Fork. One option from there would be to continue north on US 83 to I-70, and follow it east to Fort Hays and south on SH 156 to Fort Harker, then on to Salina at I-135.

Other options include: (1) continuing west from Garden City to Fort Lyon, Colorado, and the Sand Creek Massacre site; (2) driving from Scott City to Fort Wallace and on to the Battle of Beecher Island site; or (3) continuing east from Salina to Fort Riley, the Kansas Historical Society at Topeka, and Fort Leavenworth.

Notes

1. Elizabeth Custer, *Tenting on the Prairie* (New York: C. L. Webster and Co., 1889), 340.

2. Ibid., 233.

3. Ibid., 387.

CHAPTER TWELVE

Colorado Tour Guide

P lains Indian history in Colorado prior to the Gold Rush of 1858 was defined largely by the movement of northern tribes into the region to hunt, secure horses, and take up residence. The Comanches arrived first, followed by the Kiowas, both of whom had been overwhelmed by the Lakotas and other tribes in the north. The Comanches and Kiowas eventually migrated beyond the Arkansas River, combating the Apaches for entry into New Mexico and Texas. Affiliated bands of Cheyennes and Arapahos, who had split off from their northern kin, arrived to enjoy the bountiful hunting ranges of Colorado's South Park and to trade at posts established by the Bents, Ceran St. Vrain, and others along the Arkansas. A journal kept by fur trader Jacob Fowler, who was active along the Upper Arkansas in 1821, shows the region during his day to be a prime gathering place for bands from the upper Rockies to Texas.

On occasion, conflicts between the Spanish of New Mexico and the Comanches spilled over into Colorado. One such, the Battle of Greenhorn Mountain west of present Trinidad, Colorado, occurred when a Spanish army led by Gov. Don Juan Bautista de Anza entrapped and killed the noted Comanche leader Cuerno Verde. Warfare also persisted between the Utes of eastern Colorado and Plains tribes such as the Kiowas and Cheyennes.

The 1851 Treaty of Horse Creek (or Fort Laramie) officially designated the area between the Platte and Arkansas Rivers from western Kansas to the eastern range of the Rocky Mountains as the territory of the confederated Cheyenne and Arapaho tribes. The stampede of gold seekers to Colorado in 1858 and 1859 and the ensuing settlements along the eastern

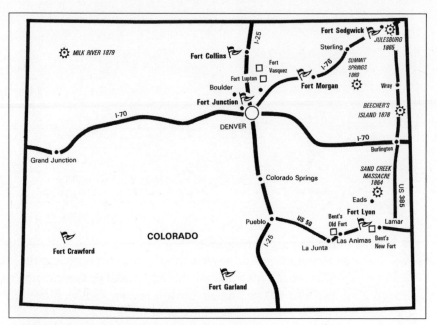

Colorado forts and battle sites. (Courtesy of author)

slopes of the Rockies ended Indian dominance of the region. The U.S. Government now looked to Colorado's great mineral wealth, and initiated a new agreement with the Cheyennes and Arapahos. Still, war came to Colorado.

Battle Sites

• **BEECHER'S ISLAND BATTLE:** Located fifteen miles east of Wray in Yuma County off US 385, the site features a small park and a stone monument bearing the names of those killed in the fight. The river island along with graves and historical markers that were once there have been moved to Wray. (See Wray Museum below.)

• **JULESBURG ATTACK:** Site of the original Julesburg and that of Fort Rankin no longer exist. Those interested in learning more regarding the Cheyenne attacks of February 2, 1865, can do so at the Fort Sedgwick Museum, 114 E. First, and at the Fort Sedgwick Depot Museum, 201 W. First. Offered are Native American artifacts, prehistoric fossils, Western paintings, weapons, and other material relative to the early period of Julesburg, the Pony Express, and the Union Pacific Railroad.

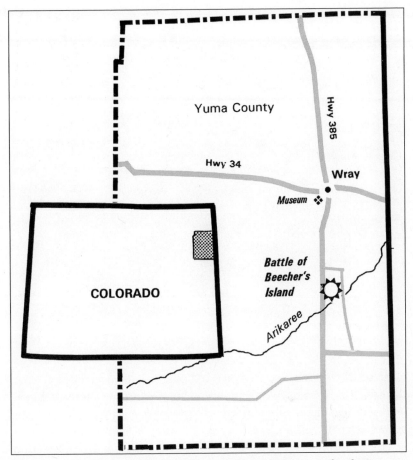

Road map to Battle of Beecher's Island/Summit Springs. (Courtesy of author)

• **SAND CREEK MASSACRE:** Because of its magnitude of injury and betrayal, Chivington's attack on Black Kettle's Cheyenne camp became a symbol of white perfidy to the Indian and a moral stain for the nation. The massacre site some thirty-five miles north of Lamar and nine miles northeast of Chivington is presently in the process of becoming a National Historic Site. An archeological survey was undertaken recently to determine the battle site's precise location.

• **SUMMIT SPRINGS BATTLE:** This engagement took place in a large ravine on the Propst ranch just west of SH 61 in northern Washington County, some twenty miles south of Sterling. A stone marker commemorates the fight.

An artist's portrayal of the Battle of Beecher's Island. (*Harper's Weekly*)

Fort Sites

• **BENT'S NEW FORT:** Erected in 1853 by William Bent on a rock bluff along the Arkansas River just west of present Lamar, to replace his former post. It became a gathering point for tribes of the surrounding region and later served as a commissary for Fort Lyon. Only the rock foundations remain, but the stone bluff is inscribed with names of soldiers and early-day travelers of the Santa Fe Trail.

• **BENT'S OLD FORT NATIONAL HISTORIC SITE:** This reconstructed fort is located on SH 194 eight miles east of La Junta. Originally called Fort William by the Bent brothers and Ceran St. Vrain who founded it in 1833, the fort was operated by William Bent as an early Indian trading post and stop on the Santa Fe Trail. Bent destroyed the fort in 1849 following an outbreak of cholera and refusal of the government to purchase it. Now under the auspices of the National Park Service, it features a museum among its twenty-four rooms of Plains Indian artifacts. Historical reenactments are conducted each Fourth of July. 719–383–5010. www.bent'soldfort.areaparks.com

• **FORT GARLAND STATE HISTORICAL MONUMENT:** Established in June 1858 at the present town of Garland to protect settlers from the

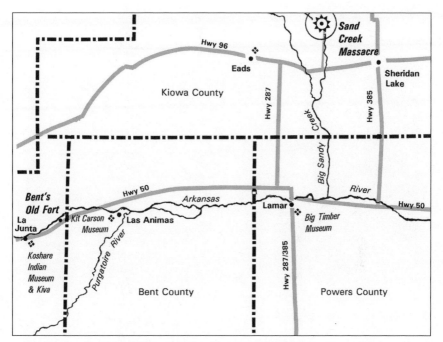

Road map to Sand Creek Massacre site. (Courtesy of author)

Utes and Jicarilla Apaches. Named for Col. John Garland, Eighth Infantry, it was abandoned on November 30, 1883. Kit Carson commanded the post in 1866. Many of the fort's adobe buildings have been restored and its commandant's quarters recreated. A museum offers displays of early military life, folk art depicting Hispanic culture, a period stagecoach, and other historical artifacts. 719–379–3512.

• **FORT LYON (ORIGINAL):** The original site, located immediately above the rock bluff of Bent's New Fort on the north bank of the Arkansas River west of Lamar, is abandoned with only structural outlines of the officers' quarters remaining. The post was constructed in August 1860 and named Fort Wise, after the governor of Virginia, Henry A. Wise. At the outbreak of the Civil War, it was renamed Fort Lyon in honor of Union general Nathaniel Lyon, who was killed in the Battle of Wilson's Creek, Missouri. In June 1867 it was moved west to the current town site of Fort Lyon on US 50, where a national cemetery is now located. The new site has served as a Naval Hospital and a VA Hospital.

Black Kettle's campsite at Sand Creek. (Author photo)

• **FORT LUPTON:** This trading post, first known as Fort Lancaster, was constructed on the South Platte in 1836 by Lt. Lancaster Lupton, a member of Col. Henry Dodge's 1835 exploring party. Abandoned in 1845, its Adobe Ruins are on private property, but a model of it and historical artifacts can be seen at the Fort Lupton Museum. 303–857–1634. www.fortlupton.org/museum

• **FORT MORGAN:** Established in July 1865 at present Fort Morgan and named for Maj. Christopher Morgan of First Illinois Cavalry to protect emigrants and transportation. Constructed of sod and logs, it was closed in May 1868. The City of Fort Morgan operates a museum at 414 Main St., displaying historical materials and artifacts of the former fort and the Cheyenne and Arapaho Indians who once resided here, as well as regional history and other subjects. 970–542–3000. www.ftmorganmus.org

• **FORT ST. VRAIN:** Established in 1837 by Ceran St. Vrain some seventeen miles south of present Greeley. For a time this trading post was the gathering and trading place of the Cheyennes and other tribes. The post was in ruins when historian Francis Parkman visited it in 1846. Thomas Fitzpatrick, mountain man turned Indian agent, delivered the first Treaty of Fort Laramie annuity goods to the Cheyennes and Arapahos there in 1852 and again in 1853. Col. E. V. Sumner consolidated his forces at Fort

St. Vrain prior to his 1857 battle with the Cheyennes on the Solomon Fork in Kansas. Gen. John C. Fremont, along with guide Kit Carson, organized his 1848 Western exploring expedition at the site that is now marked with a six-foot-tall granite slab.

• **FORT SEDGWICK/JULESBURG:** The fort's existence is celebrated through the Fort Sedgwick Museum and the Fort Sedgwick Depot Museum in Julesburg. It was established in May 1864 to protect the South Platte River migration from Indian attacks. General Sherman described Fort Sedgwick in 1866 as "three sets of company quarters made of adobe walls, with good doors and windows, but the floor and roofs are earth."[1] Constructed largely of sod with a corral and stables, the post was first called Fort Rankin. Abandoned in 1871, its site is marked today by its cemetery and a flagpole. Julesburg functioned as a Pony Express relay station for the Overland Stage Company and as a stop on the Union Pacific rail line. Fort Sedgwick Depot Museum: 970–474–2264; Fort Sedgwick Museum: 970–474–2061.

• **FORT VASQUEZ:** Established at the mouth of Clear Creek near present Platteville in the early 1830s by Louis Vasquez and Andrew Sublette, this adobe trading post with twelve-foot-high walls was still operating when Thomas Fitzpatrick visited it in 1839, but it was abandoned in 1841. The Fort Vasquez Museum, 13412 US 85, provides a reconstruction of the frontier trading center, complete with artifacts uncovered during excavations. 970–785–2832. www.coloradohistory.org/hist_sites/ft_vasquez

Related Museums

• **BOULDER:** University of Colorado Museum, University of Colorado, specializes in natural history and offers artifact collections and exhibits relative to the Rocky Mountains and adjacent regions. The museum provides three permanent galleries on paleontology, anthropology, and zoology in addition to special and traveling exhibitions. 309–938–8322. http://cumuseum.colorado.edu

• **DENVER:** Black American West Museum and Heritage Center, 301 California St., preserves the culture and history of the Afro-American who took part in the settlement and advancement of the West, including his roles as frontier soldier and cowboy. 303–292–2566. www.blackamericanwest.org

• **DENVER:** Colorado History Museum, 1300 Broadway, features collections of artifacts, historical photos, dioramas, documents, exhibits, videos, tours, and speaker's bureau at its Denver location, in addition to overseeing and supporting eleven other state museum sites. 303–866–3682. www.col-oradohistory.org/hist_sites/CHM/Colorado_History_Museum.htm

• **DENVER:** Denver Public Library Western History Collection, 10 W. Fourteenth, offers extensive library and archival material on the West with focus on social life, customs, religion, government relations, warfare, military life, and tribal history. Included also is an extensive historical photo and art collection. 303–640–6377. www.denverlibrary.org/whg

• **DENVER:** Denver Museum of Natural History, 2001 Colorado Blvd., provides extensive collections and exhibits of prehistoric life, the natural world, and Native American culture. 303–370–6387. www.dmnh.org

• **EADS:** Kiowa County Museum, Main St., offers collections of Native American arrowheads and relics in addition to artifacts of pioneer farming and ranching in the area. 719–438–2250.

• **FORT CARSON:** Third Cavalry Museum, Bldg. 2160, contains weapons, equipment, documents, and historical photographs of the Third U.S. Cavalry from 1846 on. 719–526–1368.

• **FORT COLLINS:** Fort Collins Museum, 200 Mathews St., houses collections of prehistoric Indian culture, the fur trapper period, the natural Rocky Mountain environment, and pioneer settlement. 970–316–2236. www.ci.fort-collins.co.us/museum

• **GOLDEN:** Buffalo Bill Museum and Grave, 987 1/2 Lookout Mt. Rd., features a Native American gallery along with numerous artifacts of the Western showman's life. www.buffalobill.org

• **FORT GARLAND:** Fort Garland Museum, Jct. US 160 and Colo. Hwy., provides a recreated adobe post and exhibits of frontier military life in addition to others depicting Hispanic culture of the San Luis Valley region. 719–379–3512.

• **FORT MORGAN:** Oasis of the Plains Museum, 6877 Morgan Co. Rd. 14, houses artifacts from Colorado's early Indian and settlement history. 970–432–5200.

• **KIT CARSON:** Kit Carson Historical Society, Park St., displays Native American artifacts and natural history objects. 719–962–3306.

• **LA JUNTA:** Koshare Indian Museum, 115 W. Eighteenth, maintains collections and exhibits of pottery, beadwork, quilt work, instruments, and jewelry of various American Indian tribes. 719–384–7500. www.koshare.org

• **LAMAR:** Big Timbers Museum. 7515 US 50, offers artifacts and historical photos of the region, including those relating to Native Americans. 719–336–2472. www.bigtimbers.org

• **LAS ANIMAS:** Kit Carson Museum, 305 St. Vrain, includes Native American subjects among its fifteen rooms of exhibits and collections. 719–456–2005. www.santafetrailscenicandhistoricbyway.org/kcmus.html
• **PUEBLO:** El Pueblo Museum, 324 W. First, provides a full-sized replica of the 1842 El Pueblo trading post, whose location was a crossroads for Plains tribes of its day, plus historical exhibits. 719–583–0453. www.pueblo.org/visitorsguide/museums
• **PUEBLO:** Pueblo County Historical Society Museum, 212 S. Grand Ave., features Native American artifacts and displays related to its frontier history. 719–543–6772. www.pueblohistory.org/collections
• **STERLING:** Overland Trail Museum, 21053 County Rd., exhibits a variety of historical artifacts from this region that was once the route of native Plains tribes. It features a historical village and a massive fireplace constructed of petrified wood. 970–522–3895. www.sterlingco-lo.com/parks/pr_mus
• **WRAY:** Wray Museum, 205 E. Third, is well known for its Smithsonian-created exhibit on paleo-Indians and one of the oldest bison-kill sites of the Stone Age some ten thousand years ago. One exhibit delineates the Battle of Beecher's Island, which occurred fifteen miles south of Wray. 970–332–5063. www.wrayco.net/museum

Trails to Explore

• **THE ARKANSAS RIVER TRAIL:** One Colorado route with great Plains Indian history is that along the upper Arkansas River. The first white men came to hunt, trap, and trade with the numerous Plains tribes who gathered here. The color and adventure of this period is well portrayed in *The Journal of Jacob Fowler*, ed. by Elliott Coues (Minneapolis: Ross & Haines, 1968); *Wah-To-Yah and the Taos Trail* by Lewis Garrard (Palo Alto: American West Publishing Co., 1968); and *Life in the Far West* by George F. Ruxton (Norman: University of Oklahoma Press, 1979). Eventually the Arkansas became a trading center for the tribes with the establishment of trading posts at Pueblo and on downriver by the Bent brothers and Ceran St. Vrain. Along these banks marched the first U.S. explorers as well as the early New Mexican and Missouri traders whose caravans plied the Santa Fe Trail.

Though some of the early-day sites such as the original Fort Lyon and Bent's New Fort near Lamar are no longer visible, the historical significance of the region is remembered in the Bent's Old Fort National Historic Site on US 50 just east of La Junta. A number of other local museums offer fare relating to the Plains Indians. Among them are El Pueblo Museum at Pueblo, Koshare Indian Museum at La Junta, Kit Carson Museum at Las Animas, Big Timbers Museum at Lamar, and Kiowa County Museum at Eads.

It was down the Arkansas River, too, that in November 1864 Colonel Chivington marched through the snow from Denver on his way to attack Black Kettle's camp at Sand Creek. The Sand Creek location, now a National Historic Battlefield Site, can be reached from Lamar on SH 287 and SH 96.

• **THE SOUTH PLATTE TRAIL:** Another historically rich trail in Colorado follows along the South Platte River from Nebraska to Denver. Here at the early trading posts, Indian tribes became acquainted with the white man and bartered furs for manufactured goods. The South Platte was not only the homeland and hunting grounds of the Cheyennes, Arapahos, and other Plains Indian tribes, but it was a vital avenue for westward exploration and expansion. Thousands of gold seekers flooded the route during the California Gold Rush of 1849 and again with the Pike's Peak Gold Rush of 1858 and 1859. Military expeditions, traders, and others who played a role in the state's history and the Indian wars plied the South Platte route. The Cheyennes vented their wrath following Sand Creek at Julesburg, and soon after came the hard-riding Pony Express. Custer marched his weary and thirst-driven Seventh Cavalry to the South Platte in 1866, and it was near the South Platte that Tall Bull fell to the Fifth Cavalry under Gen. Eugene A. Carr. Not far to the south in 1867, Maj. George A. Forsyth led his scouts into a deadly Cheyenne ambush on the Arikaree, resulting in the deaths of Lt. Fred Beecher and Cheyenne war leader, Roman Nose.

Other clashes of lesser magnitude remain unmarked, among them the Dunn and two Downing fights with the Cheyennes north of the South Platte west of Fort Morgan. A number of museums along the trail offer further enlightenment on this historic route.

Note

1. House of Representatives Ex. Doc. 23, 39/1: 6.

CHAPTER THIRTEEN

Nebraska Tour Guide

Nebraska was the home of the Omaha, Ponca, Otto, and Missouri tribes, all of whom resided along the Missouri River. The Pawnees held the large central area, while their traditional enemies, the Sioux, Cheyennes, and Arapahos, dominated the western Panhandle. White contact with the Plains Indians of Nebraska first occurred on two important routes west: the Missouri River waterway and the Platte River overland road. The former of these guided Lewis and Clark on their way to the Pacific Ocean. These rivers also served as a crucial water route for the early fur traders in transporting their cargoes of furs from the Rocky Mountains to the river port of St. Louis.

The Platte River road—used by fur traders, gold seekers, Mormons, military expeditions, and a multitude of settlers headed for Colorado, Oregon, California, and other Western regions—provided a colorful pageant of American commerce, exploration, and migration during the nineteenth century.

Battle Sites

• **BATTLE CREEK:** Marker on SH 121 north of town of Battle Creek. Tells story of how U.S. Dragoons under Gen. John Thayer forced the surrender of a Pawnee village in July 1859.

• **BLUEWATER:** Historical marker denoting Harney's 1855 victory over the Sioux is located on US 62 some two miles northwest of Lewellen.

• **FORT ROBINSON MASSACRE:** The Northern Cheyenne escape from their prison barracks at Fort Robinson ranks as the most dramatic of Nebraska's Indian conflicts. Beyond the killing at Fort Robinson, several battles were fought to the northwest in the pine forests that paralleled

Nebraska Forts and Battle Sites

Nebraska forts and battle sites. (Courtesy of author)

the Hat Creek Road and the final one in the death pit on Antelope Creek. None of the battle sites other than that at Fort Robinson, however, have been specifically identified and marked. The death pit, where the slain Cheyennes were buried, is considered sacred ground.

• **INDIAN WAR OF 1864:** Marker on SH 14 nine miles north of Nelson tells of Indian raids along the Oregon Trail in 1864 during which homesteads and wagon trains were attacked and looted and captives taken. Another related marker in the Oregon Trail Park at Oak, Nuckolls County, is dedicated to 16-year-old Laura Roper along with Mrs. Lucinda Eubanks and her two children who were taken captive in August 1864.

• **MASSACRE CANYON:** Monument recounting the massacre of a large Pawnee hunting party by the Sioux in 1873 is located on US 34 east of Trenton.

• **SPRING CREEK SKIRMISH:** Marker on SH 136 west of Ruskin. Relates account of five Second U.S. Cavalrymen who, while looking for lost horses, fought a two-hour skirmish with fifty Indians during May 1870.

• **WARBONNET CONFRONTATION SITE:** By following markers five miles north on SH 2 from Crawford, a traveler can reach the Warbonnet Battlefield marker atop a high knoll on a level plain. There in 1876, Merritt intercepted the Northern Cheyennes, who returned to their reservation without contest. Other than Buffalo Bill Cody's killing of Cheyenne sub-chief Yellow Hand, no fighting occurred. The final battle of the Northern

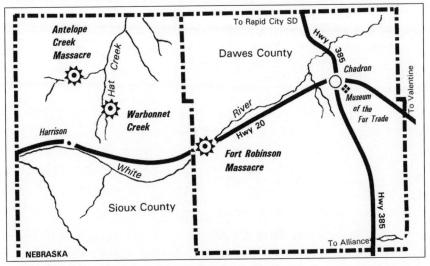

Battle sites of Northwest Nebraska. (Courtesy of author)

Cheyennes' escape from Fort Robinson was fought on nearby Antelope Creek. The site is on private property and not open to the public.

Fort Sites

• **CAMP SHERIDAN:** Camp established to monitor Spotted Tail Indian Agency that was located there briefly. Named for Gen. Phil Sheridan. It is now a Restricted Archeological Site on private land near Hays Spring.

• **FORT HARTSUFF STATE HISTORICAL PARK:** Fort Hartsuff was established September 5, 1874, to protect settlers in the region from the Brulé and Oglala Sioux. Named for Maj. Gen. George L. Hartsuff. Abandoned in May 1881, its buildings have been restored to their original condition. 308–346–4715. www.esu3.k12.ne.us/nebraska/nhm/ftharthp

• **FORT KEARNY (ORIGINAL):** Located at site of present Nebraska City. Named for Col. Stephen Watts Kearny, First U.S. Dragoons on May 23, 1846, to protect Oregon Trail transportation but was soon abandoned in May 1848.

• **FORT KEARNY STATE HISTORICAL PARK:** New Fort Kearny was established in 1848 to protect the westward immigration and to serve as a military munitions depot. It was closed in 1871. The park is located on SH 44 southeast of Kearny. After constructing the post, Colonel Kearny with fifteen hundred men marched to Santa Fe, New Mexico, where he participated in the Mexican War. The park contains a stockade, parade ground, blacksmith shop, carpenter shop, and an Interpretive Center. A slide presentation on the fort's history is provided. 308–865–5306. www.esu3.org/nebraska/ftkearny/ftkear

• **FORT MCPHERSON NATIONAL CEMETERY:** Located two miles south of I-80 Exit 190 at Maxwell, eleven miles east of North Platte. Fort McPherson was established in 1863 as Cottonwood Post. Later it became Fort Cottonwood and then Fort McPherson. Following his march to Pawnee Fork with Hancock in 1867, Custer and the Seventh Cavalry were called upon to punish the unruly tribes. Custer arrived at Fort McPherson in June, there holding a council with Sioux leader Pawnee Killer. General Sherman, who arrived at the post later, criticized Custer for not taking the Sioux prisoner, then sent him on his way into western Kansas to capture the Indians. It was a task, Custer found, far more easily ordered than accomplished. Carr was more successful in June 1869, when he marched from Fort McPherson to defeat Tall Bull's Cheyenne Dog Soldiers at Summit Springs, Colorado. Closed in 1880, the fort's structures were removed, leaving only the National Cemetery (established 1873) at its location. 308–582–4433. www.cem.va.gov/nchp/ftmcpherson

• **FORT NIOBRARA:** Established in April 1880 east of present Valentine to protect settlers from Lakota raiders and to oversee the Spotted Tail Agency. Named for the river on which it was located, it was abandoned in 1906. Its grounds are now part of a wildlife refuge. 402–376–3789.

• **FORT OMAHA:** Thirtieth and Fort Sts., features the house of Gen. George Crook, who played a prominent role in the Indian Wars of the Northern Plains and the southwest. 402–455–9990. http://omahahistory.org/fort_omaha

• **FORT ROBINSON STATE HISTORICAL SITE:** Located just west of Crawford on US 20, Fort Robinson has been kept in excellent condition by the Nebraska Historical Society, which has maintained its original officer quarters, headquarters, and other buildings. The Red Cloud Buttes dress the skyline to the north.

The restored prison barracks from which the Cheyennes escaped stands on the site of Fort Robinson, in addition to plaques detailing the Northern Cheyenne outbreak of January 1879 and the stabbing death of Lakota chief Crazy Horse at the post on September 5, 1877.

Red Cloud Agency, which temporarily stood just east of Fort Robinson proper, is indicated by plaques connoting the various agency buildings and by a Commemorative Monument. The on-site Fort Robinson Museum offers library facilities, artifacts, programs, and research files relating to the fort's history as a cavalry post and twentieth century remount station. 308–665–2919. www.nebraskahistory.org/sites/fortrob

• **FORT SIDNEY:** Located at Sidney, Nebraska. The post was first established as Camp Sidney or Sidney Barracks to protect Union Pacific railroad crews but soon evolved into an Indian War post. Today it features the post commander's quarters and the base powder magazine. A museum is operated by the Cheyenne County Historical Association. 308–254–2150.

Other Sites to See

• **AGATE FOSSIL BED NATIONAL MONUMENT:** Located on SH 29 south of Harrison, the site features the excellent Red Cloud Collection of Lakota artifacts. 308–668–2211. www.nps.gov/agfo

• **ASH HOLLOW STATE HISTORIC SITE:** Visitor center for the four-acre Ash Hollow State Historical Park is located three miles southeast of Lewellen on US 26. Ash Hollow was a camping spot of choice for countless travelers on the Platte Trail. The visitor center overlooks the Bluewater Battle Site. 308–778–5651.

• **CHIMNEY ROCK NATIONAL HISTORIC SITE:** Possibly the most famous landmark on the Platte Trail, the unique column inevitably caught the attention and admiration of early travelers. At times it was called "Nose Mountain," "the Chimney," or by the Indian name of "Elk Brick." Military explorer B. L. E. Bonneville described the column as "a conical mound, rising out of the naked plain ...about 120 feet in height...and may be seen at the distance upwards of thirty miles."[1] Visitor center: 308–586–2581. www.nps.gov/chro.

• **BAYARD CHIMNEY ROCK MUSEUM:** 308–586–1177. www.westnebraska.com/Area_Attractions/Banner_County/BayardCRMuseum

• **COURTHOUSE ROCK:** Located six miles south of Bridgeport. Also known as Solitary Rock, the Church, the Capitol, and the Castle. The precise origin of its name is unclear, but missionary Samuel Parker saw it looking like an old castle with walls, roof, turrets, embrasures, dome, windows, and large guardhouses. 308–764–2367. Jail Rock stands nearby.

• **GREAT PLATTE RIVER ROAD ARCHWAY:** Located over I-80 east of Kearney; contains exhibits devoted to the history of the Platte River Route.

• **HORSE CREEK TREATY COUNCIL SITE:** Better known as the Treaty of Fort Laramie. This momentous treaty council of 1851 was actually conducted on what is now Nebraska soil, it being moved there to provide better grazing for the thousands of Indian horses. Marker located one mile west of Morrill on US 26.

• **HUDSON-MENG BISON BONEBED:** Northwest of Crawford, features over six hundred prehistoric bison skeletons unearthed at the site. 308–432–0300. www.westnebraska.com/Area_Attractions/Dawes/Hudson-Meng.htm

• **MARI SANDOZ STATE HISTORICAL MARKER:** Located on SH 27 between Gordon and Ellsworth. Commemorates this famous Nebraska novelist, historian, and chronicler of the West. www.nebraskahistory.org/publish/markers/texts/mari_sandoz.htm

• **REPUBLICAN PAWNEE VILLAGE MARKER:** Located on SH 78 in Guide Rock, Webster County. Chronicles visit of Lt. Zebulon M. Pike to village of Republican Pawnees in 1806. Nearby is site of a Pawnee "sacred place," *Pahur* or "hill that points the way." www.nebraskahistory.org/publish/markers/texts/republican-pawnee_village.htm

Related Museums

• **CHADRON:** Museum of the Fur Trade, three miles west on US 20, reconstructed on the site of the American Fur Company's original 1837 post, features three galleries exhibiting a wide variety of fur trade paraphernalia embodied in relations with the early Plains tribes. 308–432–3843. www.furtrade.org

• **CHADRON:** Dawes County Historical Society Museum, 341 Country Club Rd., presents early history of region. 308–432–2309. www.chadron.com/memberpages/dchm

• **CHADRON:** Mari Sandoz Heritage Room, Chadron State College, Admin. Bldg., 2nd Floor. Features writing and research of Mari Sandoz. 308–432–6276. www.csc.edu/sandoz

• **CRAWFORD:** Trailside Museum of Natural History, three miles west on US 20 at Fort Robinson State Park, features paleontology and geology exhibits along with local and Native American artwork and crafts. 308–665–2929. http://trailside.unl.edu

• **FORT ROBINSON:** Fort Robinson Museum, Post HQ Bldg., exhibits trace history of the post from its military beginning and the Red Cloud Agency to the K-9 (Dog) Corps program and housing of German prisoners during World War II. The museum also holds special materials regarding the Cheyenne outbreak of 1879 and the role of Buffalo Soldiers in the Indian wars of the region. Its library contains books on military, Western, and Native American history. 308–665–2900. www.nebraskahistory.org/sites/fortrob

• **GERING:** North Platte Valley Museum, Eleventh and J, which serves as a repository for the Paul and Helen Henderson Oregon Trail Collection, offers numerous displays relating to Lakota and Cheyenne cultures, the great migrations, and the sod house and ranching settlement of the North Platte valley. 308–436–5411. www.npvm.org

• **GOTHENBURG:** Pony Express Station, 1500 Lake, features a museum and souvenir shop. 308–537–3505.

• **GOTHENBURG:** Sod House Museum, exit 211, I-80, offers a replica of a pioneer home among other items of Nebraska history. 308–537–3505.

• **KEARNEY:** Museum of Nebraska Art, 2401 Central Ave., features work by many of the famous artist-explorers of the West, plus a collection of paintings by John James Audubon. 308–865–8559. http://monet.unk.edu/mona

• **KEARNEY:** Fort Kearny Museum, 131 S. Central, offers historical and multicultural displays. 308–234–5200.

• **LINCOLN:** Nebraska State Historical Society, Fifteenth and P Sts., offers a historical museum, library, and research center with special collections, including that of Mari Sandoz. 402–471–3270. www.nebraskahistory.org

• **LINCOLN:** Great Plains Art Museum, 215 Love Library, Thirteenth and R Sts., features western art that includes sculpture by Russell and Remington. 402–472–6220. www.unl.edu/plains/gallery

• **LINCOLN:** Museum of Nebraska History, Fifteenth and P Sts., University campus, includes exhibits of Plains Indian history over twelve thousand years and other special collections of Nebraska history. 402–471–4754. www.nebraskahistory.org/sites/mnh

• **LINCOLN:** State Museum of Natural History and Mueller Planetarium, Morrill Hall, Fourteenth and U Sts., University campus, is Nebraska's largest natural history museum. 402–472–2642. www.museum.unl.edu

• **NORTH PLATTE:** Lincoln County Historical Museum, 2403 N. Buffalo Bill Ave., features a Western Heritage Village that includes the 1863 Fort McPherson Headquarters Bldg.; Union Pacific RR Depot, 1886; DAR log cabin, 1866; Pony Express log station, 1860; and tools, weapons, wagons, historical photos, and other artifacts of the Old West. 308–534–5640, 800–955–4528. http://npcanteen.tripod.com/canteen/lchm

• **NORTH PLATTE:** Buffalo Bill's "Scout's Rest Ranch" State Historical Park. Tours of showman's ranch house and barn are offered. 308–535–8035. www.ci.north-platte.ne.us/localattract.htm

• **OMAHA:** Oran's Black Americana History, 1240 S. Thirteenth, displays wax figures of prominent Black historical figures, including the Buffalo Soldier, complete with authentic clothes and uniforms in addition to the world's largest collection of Black American artifacts. 402–341–6908.

• **OMAHA:** Great Plains Black Museum, 2213 Lake Ave., provides historical displays with rare photos and relics from pre–Civil War on recounting the role of the African American in development of the American West. 402–345–2212.

• **SCOTTSBLUFF:** Scott's Bluff National Monument Interpretive Center and Oregon Trail Museum, five miles southwest of the city, offers literature and exhibits relating to the Western migration, emphasizing the natural and human history plus a collection of watercolor paintings by the frontier photographer and artist William Henry Jackson. 508–436–4340. http://scottsbluff.areaparks.com

SUPERIOR: Nuckolls County Museum, 612 E. Sixth, holds collection of American Indian artifacts, including some belonging to Chief Red Cloud. 402–879–4144/3394.

Trails to Explore

• **PLATTE RIVER TRAIL:** It would be difficult to overstate the historical significance and human drama of the Platte River Trail across southern Nebraska. The trail served as a route westward for the early fur trappers, the Oregon Trail exodus of 1842–46, the Mormons in their migration to Utah of 1846–47, the California Gold Rush of 1849–50, and the Colorado Gold Rush of 1859–60. The Platte River Trail functioned as a highway for the movement of exploring parties, military units, commercial goods, vital Rocky Mountain ores, and families seeking new homes in the West. The trail also provided a line of contact between the native Indian and the Anglo-American, sometimes on a peaceful basis and often not. Nowhere is the image of long lines of covered wagon caravans moving ever westward more applicable. The human drama of this westward exodus finds testimony in the many people who perished along the trail.

Persons taking this tour leading west on I-80 or US 30, then US 26 to Scottsbluff (see sites listed below), have two good options of continuance. One is to drive west along US 26 to the Horse Creek Treaty site and on to the Fort Laramie National Historic Site in Wyoming. Another is to turn north on SH 71 at Scottsbluff and tour the pine-clad woods country of Fort Robinson State Historical Park and other historical sites.

• **FORT ROBINSON TRAIL:** Fort Robinson, the north end of the famous Northern Cheyenne retreat of 1878, was linked to Fort Reno, Oklahoma, at the south end of the retreat in terms of its cavalry garrison and the officers and men who served at both posts. It was at Fort Robinson that Dull Knife and his people, rather than again being driven from their native homeland, made their desperate break for freedom at midwinter with many of them being killed by U.S. troops.

Chadron features the Mari Sandoz High Plains Heritage Center at Chadron State College, the Dawes County Museum, and the Museum of the Fur Trade, located on US 20 east of Chadron. Continuing east to Rushville, the traveler can learn the story of Camp Sheridan and Spotted Tail Agency at the Sheridan County Historical Museum. From here, travelers can drive north to the Pine Ridge Agency of South Dakota and the Battle of Wounded Knee site.

• **NEBRASKA SAND HILLS TRAIL:** US 20 heads eastward to SH 27 at Gordon (featuring the Cowboy Museum, Scamaborn Museum, and Mari Sandoz Room), then goes south through the Nebraska Sand Hills to Ellsworth on what has been designated as the Mari Sandoz Sand Hills Trail. A trip through the Sand Hills provides insight as to why U.S. troops were unable to locate the Northern Cheyennes during the winter of 1878–1879. The Mari Sandoz State Historical Marker is located en route to Ellsworth.

Note

1. Merrill J. Mattes, *The Great Platte River Road* (Lincoln: Nebraska Historical Society, 1969), 384.

CHAPTER FOURTEEN

Wyoming Tour Guide

Historically Wyoming was home to the Sioux, Cheyenne, Arapaho, Arikara, Bannock, Blackfeet, Crow, Gros Ventre, Kiowa, Nez Percé, Sheep Eater, Shoshone, and Ute Indians. American and French fur traders became acquainted with these tribes and the region during the early nineteenth century. Despite occasional personal eruptions, the mountain men generally maintained peaceful relations with the tribes, some of them taking Indian women as wives and siring families with them. Further, the traders began the introduction of manufactured goods among the tribes through the supply trains brought to the annual rendezvous by Missouri merchants. Among those goods were explosive weapons that the tribes employed for both hunting and warfare. Soon enough, such weapons would be turned to the defense of Indian lands against the multitude of white intruders who poured westward over the Platte River trail.

The saga of the Bozeman Trail and Red Cloud's defense of the Sioux and Northern Cheyenne Wyoming homelands against the armies of Connor, Crook, MacKenzie, and other U.S. generals is a dramatic chapter in the Indian wars. Key events of the war include the Indian's victory over Capt. William J. Fetterman and the Northern Cheyenne defeat at the hands of Mackenzie at Red Fork. The 1851 Treaty of Horse Creek near Fort Laramie stands out as one of the great peace-making festivals of the West.

Battle Sites

• **CONNOR BATTLEFIELD STATE PARK AND HISTORIC SITE:** Pyramid Monument, located in park at Ranchester on US 14 just west off I-90 Exit, marks Gen. P. E. Connor's Tongue River attack on an Arapaho village

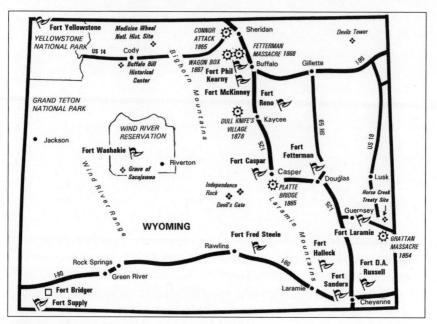

Wyoming forts and battle sites. (Courtesy of author)

under Chief Black Bear. Contact Fort Phil Kearny, 307–684–7629, www.philkearny.vcn.com, or Parks & Historic Sites, 307–777–6323.

• **FETTERMAN MASSACRE MONUMENT:** Located between Buffalo and Sheridan. Turn west off I-25 at Exit 44, drive north on US 87, and follow road markers to site. The monument is situated atop a high ridge overlooking the broad valley into which Captain Fetterman and his command were lured by the Sioux and Cheyennes and massacred to the last man.

• **GRATTAN MASSACRE SITE:** Marker on US 26, three miles west of Lingle (see account of this massacre in Chapter 3).

• **DULL KNIFE BATTLE SITE:** Undeveloped site of Col. Ranald Mackenzie's early morning attack against Dull Knife on Red Fork of the Powder River is located west of Kaycee and north of Barnum.

• **SAWYER EXPEDITION FIGHT:** Marker two miles east of Dayton on US 14. Wagon train of Bozeman Trail builder Col. J. A. Sawyer and military escort fought off attack by Arapaho Indians for thirteen days during the fall of 1865 with loss of an officer and two drovers who are buried in a common, unmarked grave at the site.

• **WAGON BOX FIGHT:** Turn west off I-90 at Exit 44 between Buffalo and Sheridan to SH 195, drive northwest beyond entrance to Fort Phil Kearny Visitor Center, and follow road markers to site south of Story.

Fort Sites

• **FORT BONNEVILLE:** Established three miles northwest of Daniel by Capt. B. L. E. Bonneville in 1832. No longer in existence.

• **FORT CASPAR:** The site of Fort Caspar, Wyoming, was originally a Mormon crossing point of the Platte and was known for several years as the Mormon Ferry. The ferry and later a thousand-foot log bridge built in 1859 were used by many emigrant trains headed west. The U.S. Government built its small adobe post there in 1858, which was attacked by the Cheyennes and Sioux in 1865. After the fort was abandoned in 1867 in favor of Fort Fetterman, it and the bridge were burned by the Indians. Though named "Caspar" for Lt. Caspar Collins who was killed there, common spelling led to the title "Casper" for the town that developed at the location. Today the Fort Caspar Museum complex incorporates a museum building and extensive post reconstruction. The museum offers a variety of exhibits on Indian, civilian, and military life of the region. The reconstructed fort includes a sutler's store, blacksmith shop, corral, commissary, squad rooms, mess hall, carriage shed, cemetery, replica of the Mormon Ferry, and support cribs for the bridge across the North Platte built by Louis Guinard in 1859. 307–235–8462. www.fortcasparwyoming.com

• **FORT FETTERMAN:** Located on SH 93 at Orpha, near the junction of the Platte River and Bozeman Trails. Two of its original buildings still stand, one of them, the officers' quarters, now serving as a museum. Established in March 1867, it operated as base for Crook's ill-fated campaign against the Sioux and Northern Cheyennes in 1876 and was used by Crook to regroup his forces. Mackenzie marched with Crook from Fort Fetterman to his victory over Dull Knife at Red Fork. After the post was abandoned in 1886, a ranch and freighting town developed at the site. Signs on the grounds describe the fort's buildings and activities, while two of the buildings house maps, drawings, photographs, and dioramas. 307–684–7629. http://wyoparks.state.wy.us/FFslide.htm

• **FORT FRED STEELE:** Established by Col. R. I. Dodge in June 1868, who named it for Maj. Gen. Frederick Steele of Civil War fame. Located on Seminoe Dam Route off I-80 east of Rock Springs and Sinclair. Its original purpose was to guard the Union Pacific Railroad from Indian attack.

It was abandoned in 1886 and transferred to the Interior Department in 1886. 307–320–3013. http://wyoparks.state.wy.us/fsslide.htm

• **FORT LARAMIE NATIONAL HISTORIC SITE:** Located three miles off US 26 from town of Fort Laramie. This celebrated fur trading center, Oregon Trail stop, and Indian War post is now a National Historic Site. A painting by artist A. J. Miller, who visited the post in 1837, reveals the exterior grounds of the fort busy with tepees and Indian life. Most of the great names of the mountain man and fur trade era found respite at Fort Laramie: Jim Bridger, Thomas Fitzpatrick, Milton Sublette, Robert Campbell, Jedediah Smith, and many others. Though its restoration is ongoing, a number of Fort Laramie's original buildings have been returned to their original state. Its centerpiece is the post headquarters and bachelor officers' quarters known as Old Bedlam. Also featured are officers' quarters, sutler's store, bakery, powder magazine, cavalry barracks, and the former commissary that now serves as a visitor center. Its museum displays Plains Indian, archeological, and military artifacts as well as many photographs of the troops and civilians who played roles in the fort's history. 307–837–2221. www.nps.gov/fola

• **FORT HALLECK:** Founded in July 1862 on north side of Elk Mountain south of I-80 between present Laramie and Rawlins to protect the Overland Trail Stage Line. Named for Maj. Gen. Henry W. Halleck, it was transferred to the Interior Department in 1886. One building, believed to be the blacksmith's shop, remains. Post cemetery was marked by the DAR in 1914.

• **FORT MCKINNEY:** Named for Lt. John A. McKinney, Fourth Cavalry, who was killed at the battle of Red Fork, the post was established in October 1876 some three miles from Fort Reno. It was moved in 1877 to its current location west of present Buffalo to control Indians in the region. The post was abandoned in 1894, and the State Soldiers' and Sailors' Home was located there. One original barracks and hospital building remain.

• **FORT PHIL KEARNY:** Take Exit 44 off I-80 between Sheridan and Buffalo. Known first as Fort Carrington, this post was built in 1866 to guard the Bozeman Trail against attacks by the Sioux and Northern Cheyennes. The main fort was six hundred by eight hundred feet, surrounded by an eight-foot stockade of pine logs with blockhouses at two diagonal corners. The Fetterman Massacre of December 1866 and continued attacks by the Indians led to abandonment of the fort by the Treaty of Fort Laramie in 1868 and its destruction by the Indians soon after. Located near Story, fifteen miles north of present Buffalo at the base of the Little

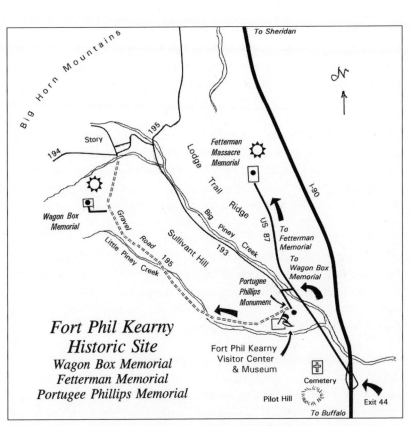

Diagram of Fort Phil Kearney Historic Area. (Courtesy of author)

Bighorn Mountains, it is now a State Historic Site. The site features a monument to Portugee Phillips, who made the heroic ride to Fort Laramie. The Fort Kearny Museum addresses the Fetterman Massacre, Connors fight, and Wagon Box battle as well as Bozeman Trail conflicts. 307–684–7629. www.philkearny.vcn.com

• **FORT RENO:** Originally established as Camp Connor on the banks of the Powder River in August 1865 as a supply base for General Connor's campaign against the Sioux and to ward off Indian attacks on the Bozeman Trail, the log stockade fort was abandoned in 1868 and later burned by the Indians. Located on SH 192 east of I-25, only soil outlines of the fort remain near Sussex. A state historical marker stands at the site.

• **FORT DAVID A. RUSSELL:** Established three miles from present Cheyenne to serve as a military supply depot and to protect construction crews of the Union Pacific Railroad in 1867, it was named for Brig. Gen. David A. Russell killed in the Battle of Opequon, Virginia. In 1930 it was renamed Fort Francis E. Warren, after the U.S. Senator from Cheyenne, and became first a Quartermaster Center and then an Air Force base in 1947. None of the original buildings exist, but those of 1885 construction remain. Museum: 307–773–2980.

• **FORT SANDERS:** Established three miles south of present Laramie in July 1866 to protect the Overland Trail and Union Pacific Railroad. First named Fort Buford, after Maj. Gen. John Buford, in 1866 it was redesignated as Fort Sanders for Brig. Gen. William P. Sanders, who was killed in the Battle of Knoxville. Abandoned in May 1882, it was transferred to the Interior Department in August of that year. Only the original guardhouse remains.

Other Sites to See

• **DEVIL'S TOWER:** Located on SH 24 in far northeastern Wyoming, this 1,267-foot vertical monolith became the nation's first national monument when declared such by President Theodore Roosevelt on September 24, 1906. It has long been a religious shrine for many Indian tribes. 307–467–5283. www.nps.gov/deto

• **FORT LARAMIE TREATY SITE:** See Horse Creek Treaty Council under Other Sites to See in Nebraska.

• **GUERNSEY:** Oregon Trail wagon ruts provide visible evidence of the many thousand ox-drawn wagons that passed along the Platte or Oregon Trail. Guernsey State Park Museum, 307–836–2334. http://wyoparks.state.wy.us/GUslide.htm

• **INDEPENDENCE ROCK STATE HISTORIC SITE:** Located on SH 220 fifty-three miles southwest of Casper. Many Oregon Trail emigrants blazed their names on the 193-foot-tall landmark. 307–577–5150. wyoparks.state.wy.us/irslide.htm or www.independence-rock.org

• **MEDICINE WHEEL NATIONAL HISTORIC SITE:** Some tourists will find it worth their time to drive west on Alt. US 14 from the Connor Battlefield site at Ranchester some sixty miles to the Medicine Wheel National Historic Site. Here on Medicine Mountain overlooking the Bighorn Basin is a great stone-laid Medicine Wheel with twenty-eight spokes and a circumference of 245 feet. This prehistoric stone shrine constructed by an unknown people is highly regarded by Native Americans today as a religious emblem of their heritage. Though still embedded with mystery, the Medicine Wheel is a reminder of those native people who existed in America prior to recorded history.

Related Museums

• **BIGHORN:** Bozeman Trail Museum, South end of Johnson St. (weekends). Housed in blacksmith shop featuring local memorabilia. www.museumsusa.org/museums/info/1165098

• **BIGHORN:** Bradford Brinton Memorial Museum, 239 Brinton Road, features Western art, rare books, artifacts, and documents relating to Native American life. 307–672–3137. http://wyshs.org/mus-brinton.htm

• **BUFFALO:** Jim Gatchell Museum, 100 Fort St., is dedicated to the history and culture of the Powder River/Bozeman Trail Region. 307–684–9331. www.jimgatchell.com

• **CHEYENNE:** Frontier Days Old West Museum, 4610 N. Carey Ave., reveals the drama and romance of the Old West through exhibits, educational programs, and research materials. 307–778–1415. www.old-westmuseum.org

• **CHEYENNE:** State Tourism Information Center, I-25 at College Drive. Assists Wyoming tourists with data on Wyoming history and exploration of the State's historic sites. 800–225–5996 or 307–777–7777. www.wyomingtourism.org

• **CHEYENNE:** Wyoming State Museum, 2301 Central Ave., Barrett Bldg., tells the story of Wyoming's human and natural history through its collections of Native American, military, frontier, and other artifacts. 307–777–7022. http://wyomuseum.state.wy.us

• **CODY:** Buffalo Bill Historical Center, 720 Sheridan Ave., includes five major museums: Whitney Gallery of Western Art; Buffalo Bill Museum; Cody Firearms Collection; Plains Indian Museum; and the Draper Museum of Natural History. The Center also houses the McCracken Research Library. Many famous Western artists are featured. 307–587–4771. www.bbhc.org

• **KAYCEE:** Hoofprints of the Past Museum, 344 Nolan Ave., provides the Hole-in-the-Wall Tour in June, which includes a site where early Indian writing has long been preserved. 307–738–2381. http://wyshs.org/mus-hoofprints.htm

• **MOUNTAIN VIEW:** Fort Bridger State Historic Site features several restored buildings of the old trading post and military fort in addition to a Museum and Archeological Interpretive Center. 307–782–3842. http://wyoparks.state.wy.us/FBslide.htm

• **SHERIDAN:** Historic Sheridan Inn, Fifth and Broadway, originally built in 1893 as home of William F. "Buffalo Bill" Cody. www.sheridaninn.com

Trails to Explore

• **THE PLATTE/BOZEMAN TRAIL:** The route of US 26 from the Nebraska border to I-25 and I-90 northward through Wyoming to Montana provides a historical aorta into the heart of the Plains Indian Wars north of the Platte River. Along this Wyoming trace where armies marched are the sites of the Horse Creek (Fort Laramie) Treaty of 1851, the Grattan Massacre, Fort Laramie, Fort Fetterman, Fort Caspar, the Platte Bridge fight, Old Fort Reno, Fort Phil Kearny, the Fetterman Massacre, the Wagon Box Fight Site, and Connor's Battlefield Site. Even as events of the Indian Wars led participants on into Montana, a historically interested traveler may well wish to continue north to visit sites there, especially that of Custer's defeat at the Little Bighorn. The tour provides Western scenic advantage and thus many excellent photo opportunities.

In addition to its forts and battle sites, the Bozeman Trail route offers historic places of interest such as Horseshoe Station, where Portugee Phillips wired news of the Fetterman Massacre; Jim Bridger's Ferry, starting point of the Bozeman Trail; Deer Creek Station; Richard's Bridge; Cooke's 17 Miles Stage Station; and the Powder River Crossing, seven miles west of which a train of 150 wagons and 467 people was attacked by a Lakota and Cheyenne war party.

CHAPTER FIFTEEN

Montana Tour Guide

A s with other mountain states, Montana's history features early contact by the fur traders, missionaries, and government explorers. Though preceded by French traders from Canada, Lewis and Clark made the first U.S. entry in 1805. Trader Manuel Lisa arrived soon after, building a trading post at the mouth of the Bighorn River in 1807 and beginning two decades of fur trade operation on the Yellowstone. These and other Americans who ventured into the Montana region found the pro-Canadian Blackfoot and Piegan Indians to be dangerous enemies to American interests. The American Fur Company established Fort Union on the Missouri River at the present Montana–North Dakota line in 1829 and Fort Benton at the head of Missouri River navigation in 1846.

Even as the fur trade died out, the revelation of gold discoveries in Montana in 1858 spawned a boom of mining camps that evolved into towns such as Virginia City and Helena. The transportation of ores eastward, along with developing agricultural and ranching operations, created great pressure on the government to safeguard roads through lands held by the Indian tribes. The Northern Overland road to Minnesota and the Bozeman Trail into Wyoming were of principal concern.

Battle Sites

• **BEAR PAW BATTLE SITE:** The surrender of Chief Joseph and his Nez Percé is recorded in on-site monuments located on SH 240 sixteen miles south from Chinook. It was here that Nez Percé Chief Joseph uttered his famous words: "From where the sun now stands, I will fight no more forever." 406–357–2590. www.friendsnezpercebattlefields.org

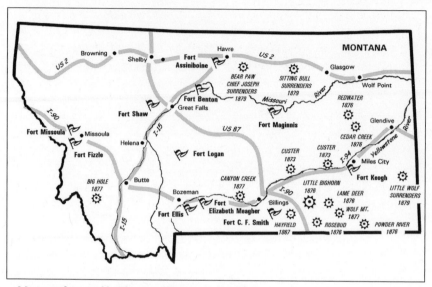

Montana forts and battle sites. (Courtesy of author)

• **BIG HOLE NATIONAL BATTLEFIELD,** Nez Percé National Historical Park: Museum and visitor center, north side of SH 43 between Chief Joseph Pass and Wisdom, overlooks the site of the Nez Percé battle with forces under Col. John Gibbon. The museum displays photographs and personal artifacts of participants, and a tour of the battle site can be made. 406–689–3155. www.nps.gov/biho

• **CANYON CREEK BATTLE SITE:** Located off I-90 west of Billings and north of Laurel. Though the site is on private property, a monument provides information regarding this unsuccessful attempt by Col. Samuel D. Sturgis to stop the Nez Percés' flight to Canada. Pioneer Museum, Billings: 406–256–6809.

• **CROOK'S ROSEBUD BATTLE SITE:** This battle site is situated in the Rosebud Battlefield State Park off SH 314 north of Decker. Here the Sioux under Crazy Horse and Northern Cheyenne warriors turned back Crook's expedition in an all-day battle on June 17, 1876, just prior to the Little Bighorn massacre. Historical markers provide details as to the action and location.

• **HAYFIELD BATTLE SITE:** Located on private land in the Bighorn Canyon National Recreation Area. Here a large party of Northern Cheyennes and Sioux were held off by a hay-gathering party of a few soldiers and civilians who were armed with breech-loading Springfield rifles. Pioneer Museum, Billings: 406–256–6809.

• **LAME DEER BATTLE SITE AND CEMETERY:** This central settlement of the Northern Cheyenne reservation contains two items of special historical interest. As noted by a historical monument in the town, it was at Lame Deer that General Miles defeated a band of Miniconjou Sioux and killed Chief Lame Deer. Moreover, two of the Northern Cheyennes' greatest chiefs, Dull Knife (or Morning Star) and Little Wolf, are buried in the Lame Deer Cemetery. These two men helped lead their people back north from the Indian Territory (Oklahoma) in 1878.

• **LITTLE BIGHORN BATTLEFIELD NATIONAL SITE:** This premiere Indian battle site is located to the east of I-90 off SH 212. Central feature of the site is the Little Bighorn Monument on the hill where Custer and over 215 of his men perished on June 25, 1876. This is supported by a visitor center, museum, trails, group tours, and historical interpreters, plus the Custer Battlefield National Cemetery. Indian and Seventh Cavalry artifacts excavated on site and extensive dioramas let visitors relive this most-famous-of-all cavalry/Indian conflict. Paved trails permit auto tours of the Reno-Benteen engagement and follow Custer's very march to his final contest with the Indians. A monument dedicated to the Sioux and Cheyennes who participated in this great Indian victory will soon join one that remembers the white soldiers who died there. 406–638–2000. www.nps.gov/libi

• **POWDER RIVER BATTLE SITE:** On March 17, 1876, a Northern Cheyenne village was attacked and burned by Col. Joseph J. Reynolds of Crook's command four miles northeast of Moorhead, where a historical marker for the site is located.

• **RENO-BENTEEN BATTLEFIELD MEMORIAL:** The battle site where Reno and Benteen fought off the Sioux and Northern Cheyennes for two days is located at and associated with the Little Bighorn site. A trail leads around the hill position where they made their defense on June 25 and 26, 1876.

• **STANLEY/CUSTER EXPEDITION OF 1873 (UNMARKED SITES):** During this campaign Custer clashed with Sioux warriors north of the Yellowstone on two occasions: near the mouth of the Tongue River on August 4 and near the mouth of the Bighorn River on August 11.

• **WOLF MOUNTAIN BATTLE SITE:** The site of Miles's January 8, 1877, attack on a camp of Oglalas and Northern Cheyennes is located on private land west of Otter and southeast of Birney in the Custer National

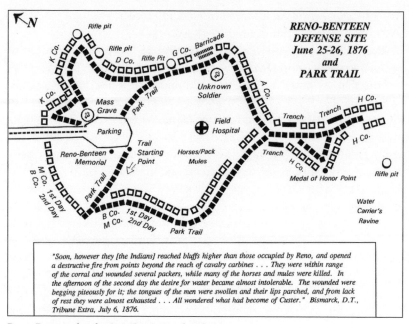

Reno-Benteen battle site. (Courtesy of author)

Forest. A state historical marker on the road near the site indicates the precise location of the battle.

Fort Sites

• **FORT ASSINIBOINE:** The fort was established in 1879 to oversee the Blackfeet and other Indians of the region and to guard against the return of Sitting Bull from Canada. Located ten miles southwest of Havre off US 87, it is now a State Historic Site and an Agricultural Research Center.

• **FORT BELKNAP:** Established in 1871 as a Northwest Fur Company Trading Post at present Chinook, its name was taken for the Fort Belknap Indian Agency thirty miles to the east. The post closed in 1886. Blaine County Museum: 406–357–2590.

• **FORT BENTON:** First constructed as a fur-trading post by the American Fur Company in 1845 and named for Missouri senator Thomas H. Benton, it became a military post in December 1850. The post was abandoned in May 1881 and its military reservation assigned to the Interior Department in January 1883. Today the Fort Benton Heritage Complex provides information and exhibits regarding the Blackfeet Indians, the visit of Lewis and Clark, and the fur and robe trade of the Upper Missouri. 406–622–5316. www.fortbenton.com

• **FORT CUSTER:** This post at the confluence of the Bighorn and Little Bighorn Rivers was established in 1877 following the Little Bighorn battle by Lt. Col. George P. Buell and operated until April 1898. Nothing of the post remains today.

• **FORT ELIZABETH MEAGHER:** This stockade post eight miles east of present Bozeman was named for the wife of Thomas F. Meagher, then acting governor of Montana. It was established in May 1867 to protect settlers of the Gallatin Valley following the murder of John Bozeman. No remains or marker exists.

• **FORT ELLIS:** Established in August 1867 three miles west of present Bozeman to protect settlers and miners from Indians of the region. It was named for Col. Augustus Van Horn Ellis who was killed at Gettysburg. Fort Ellis was abandoned in 1886 and transferred to the Interior Department. See Bozeman's Gallatin Pioneer Museum (below) regarding a model reproduction of Fort Ellis.

• **FORT KEOGH:** Located two miles southwest of the Yellowstone/Tongue River junction. It was established by General Miles in 1877 and served as his base of operations for several expeditions against the Sioux and Northern Cheyennes. Fort Keogh remained active until 1908 when it served as a livestock experiment station for a time and as a quartermaster's depot.

• **FORT LOGAN:** Established seventeen miles northwest of present White Sulphur Springs in November 1869 to protect freight routes and mining camps from the Blackfeet and other tribes. Named for Capt. William Logan, Seventh U.S. Infantry, the fort was abandoned in July 1890.

• **FORT MISSOULA:** This former post located at present Missoula was established in 1877 to protect settlers following the Nez Percé uprising. Today many of its original buildings are utilized by the National Guard and U.S. Forest Service. Its Historical Museum, Bldg. 322, records Fort Missoula's history, including its Buffalo Soldier period, and provides exhibits on early settlement and regional history. 406–728–3476. www.fortmissoulamuseum.org

• **FORT PECK:** Established in 1867 at present Fort Peck, Montana, at mouth of Milk River. Lewis and Clark encountered grizzly bears here in 1805. Site became agency for Assiniboine and Sioux Indians in May 1888, its reservation extending 110 miles along the Missouri River. The Fort Peck Dam was completed in 1938. An Interpretive Center and Museum on SH 24 offers special exhibits on Native American culture and dinosaur fossils. Center and Museum: 406–526–3431.

• **FORT C. F. SMITH:** This short-lived Bozeman Trail fort located on SH 313 near present Yellowtail on the Crow Indian reservation was established in August 1866. It was named in honor of Gen. C. F. Smith, who died on the Tennessee River in 1862. The fort was abandoned on July 29, 1868, under agreements of the Treaty of Fort Laramie in 1868. None of its structures still stand. Lt. George H. Palmer described the fort in 1867:

> About three acres of ground were enclosed by a stockade made of logs twelve feet long, set to the ground close together and having their tops sharpened. Inside of the stockade were built, for quarters for officers and men, rough log huts with dirt roofs and floors.
> — Lt. George H. Palmer, Dec. 19, 1867[1]

Other Sites to See

• **PRYOR:** Chief Plenty Coups Museum and Historic Home, located in Chief Plenty Coups State Park within the Crow Reservation, reflect the efforts of Crow chief Plenty Coups in directing his people to accept the lifestyle of the white man. 406–252–1289. www.nezperce.com/pcmain

• **PICTOGRAPH CAVES STATE PARK:** Located just east of Billings. Take Exit 452 from I-90 and follow Coburn Rd. south to site. This series of caves features painted images and artifacts of Indian hunters dating back five thousand years. 406–245–0227 or 406–247–2940. www.pictographcave.org

Related Museums

• **HELENA:** Montana Historical Society. Its museum provides information and exhibits on Indian history and U.S. military operations. A special attraction is the Charles M. Russell art collection. 406–444–2694. www.his.state.mt.us

• **BIG TIMBER:** Crazy Mountain Museum, Exit 367, Cemetery Rd., provides history of Montana's Sweetgrass Country. 406–932–5126.

• **BILLINGS:** Western Heritage Center, 2822 Montana Ave., presents the history of the Yellowstone Valley with exhibits depicting the culture of both its Native American tribes and white homesteaders. 406–256–6809. www.ywhc.org

• **BOZEMAN:** Gallatin Pioneer Museum, 317 W. Main St., offers historic artifacts that include crafts by Indians of the Northern Plains, plus a

model reproduction of Fort Ellis as it once existed nearby. 406–522–8122. www.pioneermuseum.org
• **BOZEMAN:** Museum of the Rockies, S. Seventh and Kagy Blvd. Planetarium and natural history, including Plains Indian and pioneer exhibits. 406–994–2682. www.montana.edu/wwwmor
• **BROWNING:** Museum of the Plains Indians, jct. US 2 and US 89 west of Browning, features collections of historic tribal art of the Northern Plains, multimedia presentations, dioramas, carved wood panels by Blackfeet sculptor John Clark, and murals by Blackfeet artist Victor Pepion. The museum is operated by the Arts and Crafts Board of the U.S. Department of Interior. 406–723–7211. www.doi.gov/iacb/museums/museum_plains
• **CHINOOK:** Blaine County Museum, 501 Indiana Ave., displays exhibits of Indian culture and paleontology, with special emphasis on the Battle and Siege of the Bear Paw. 406–357–2590.
• **COLUMBUS:** Museum of the Beartooths, 440 E. Fifth Ave. North, provides displays, books, and resource material on the history of the Beartooth region, including its early tribes, the mountain men fur traders, ranchers, miners, farmers, and other pioneers. 406–322–4588.
• **GREAT FALLS:** The C. M. Russell Museum Complex, 400 Thirteenth Street North, displays Russell's original log cabin studio where the famous artist produced much of his renowned Western art, as well as a large collection of his art in an adjacent museum building. 406–727–8787. www.cmrussell.org
• **GREAT FALLS:** Lewis & Clark National Historic Trail Interpretive Center, Giant Springs Road, provides live programs and videos illustrating the historic exploration of Lewis and Clark along with an on-site view of the terrain the explorers encountered along the Great Falls of the Missouri River. 406–727–8733. www.fs.fed.us/r1/lewisclark/lcic
• **HARDIN:** Bighorn County Historical Museum Complex and National Recreation Area, one mile east of Hardin, houses historical displays in twenty buildings focusing on the American Indian and pioneer settlement of the region. The visitor center is state operated. 406–665–1671. http://museumonthebighorn.org
• **LIVINGSTON:** Park County Museum, 118 W. Chinook, offers a Native Cultures room along with exhibits on Indian history, early exploration, railroading, mining, and white settlement. 406–222–4184.
• **LIVINGSTON:** Yellowstone Gateway Museum, 118 W. Chinook, includes Indian and pioneer historical displays. 406–222–4148. www.livingston-museums.org/pcm

• **RED LODGE:** Peaks to Plains Museum, 224 N. Broadway, features a Western firearms collection, along with the Greenough Rodeo Collection, coal mine exhibit, and highlights of the historic Red Lodge. 406–446–3667.

Trails to Explore

Visitors to the Little Bighorn Battlefield National Site west off of I-90 south of Hardin can extend their interest in this classic cavalry-Indian battle by taking US 212 to Lame Deer, then turning north on SH 39 to I-94, and following Custer's march along the Yellowstone northeast via Miles City and Glendive to the origin of the Seventh Cavalry's march at Fort Abraham Lincoln, Bismarck, North Dakota.

Those interested in tracing a picturesque portion of the Lewis and Clark expedition can follow I-94 from the Little Bighorn site to Billings. From there, a drive west on I-90 to Three Forks traces the epic journey of Lewis and Clark along the Yellowstone River, providing stops at Park City, Columbus, Reedpoint, Big Timber, Livingston, Bozeman, Belgrade, and Three Forks, all of which abound with historical museums as well as numerous points of sport recreation and scenery. Also on this route, just north of Laurel, is the Canyon Creek Battle Site where the U.S. Cavalry engaged the Nez Percé under Chief Joseph.

Another major battlefield in the Promethean effort of the Nez Percé to escape to Canada can be witnessed by continuing west on I-90 to Butte and following I-15 and scenic route SH 43 to the Big Hole National Battlefield. From Butte I-90 continues on to Fort Missoula at Missoula.

A trip westward along US 2 across northern Montana will take a visitor through the Fort Peck Indian Reservation; the Fort Belknap Indian Reservation; the Bear Paw Battle Site off SH 240 south of Chinook; Fort Assiniboine off US 87 south of Havre; and the Blackfeet Indian Reservation.

Potential visitors to Montana can obtain a free 35"x18" highway map by calling 800–847–4868.

Note

1. Jerome A. Greene, "Lt. Palmer Writes from the Bozeman Trail, 1867–68," *Montana Magazine* 28 (Summer 1978): 21.

CHAPTER SIXTEEN

North Dakota
Tour Guide

The first and only military operation conducted in North Dakota by the United States resulted from the Sioux uprising in Minnesota in 1862. At the request of the governor of that state, a two-pronged campaign was launched to pursue and punish the Indian culprits who had fled westward into the Dakotas.

Battle of Big Mound

One arm of the strike was commanded by Brig. Gen. Henry Hastings Sibley, who led a force of some three thousand volunteers to drive the Sioux toward the Missouri River. There, it was planned, another twelve-hundred-man force under Brig. Gen. Alfred Sully would intercept and capture them. On July 24, 1863, Sibley reached the Big Mound plateau within a hundred miles of present Bismarck. There he came onto an encampment of nearly a thousand Sisseton and Wahpeton Dakotas led by Chief Standing Buffalo, who had not taken part in the Minnesota uprising. Dr. Josiah Weiser, who was with Sibley's command, spoke the Sioux tongue. As he was aiding in a parley with the Indians, Weiser was suddenly shot and killed by a tribesman. A battle immediately erupted as the Indians dashed for cover. Sibley's artillery drove them into the open while his cavalry attempted to block their retreat westward. But the majority of the band managed to escape, some southwestward to Dead Buffalo Lake and others northward to Canada.

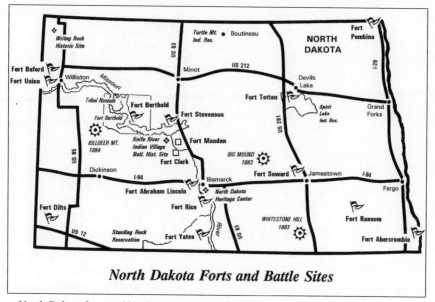

North Dakota Forts and Battle Sites

North Dakota forts and battle sites. (Courtesy of author)

Battle of White Stone Hill

It was fall before Sully's army reached North Dakota and found a Dakota village camped at White Stone Hill near present Merricourt. On September 3, he attacked the camp, and in a bloody, thirty-minute fight, by his claim, killed nearly 200 Indians, wounded 150, and captured 158. In addition, he seized large supplies of buffalo meat and a sizable number of ponies, robes, and furs. Sully then had his men destroy some five hundred of the Dakota's lodges. U.S. losses were twelve men killed and twenty-three wounded.

Battle of Killdeer Mountain

Sully led his force on to Fort Pierre and eventually from there up the Missouri with the agenda of both punishing the Sioux and developing routes to the Montana gold fields. On July 28, 1864, he discovered and attacked several groups of Dakota, Lakota, and Nakota Indians at Killdeer Mountain in far northwestern North Dakota, ten and one-half miles northwest of Killdeer. Few of the Indians, if any, are believed to have participated in the Minnesota attacks. Sitting Bull was among the chiefs present. The site marker reads:

Sully's force, equipped with several cannons, attacked
and shelled the encampment, causing warriors, as well
as unarmed men, women, and children, to flee into the
Little Missouri badlands. Native American oral tradition
says that many of these people escaped through an
opening at the top of Killdeer Mountain known as the
Medicine Hole.

Five of Sully's men were killed. Again he had the entire village
destroyed before marching across the badlands to Fort Union, skirmish-
ing with Sioux warriors on the way.

Battle Sites
• **BIG MOUND BATTLEFIELD:** Sibley's July 24, 1863, victory over a large
force of peaceful Sisseton Sioux who were conducting a buffalo hunt is
remembered with a state marker and a rock monument indicating the
place where Dr. Weiser was killed by warriors during a preliminary parley. The site is located nine miles north of I-94 at Tappen off Co. Rd. 71.
• **KILLDEER MOUNTAIN BATTLEFIELD:** This battle site in western North
Dakota is located west of Killdeer north off SH 200. Here on July 28, 1864,
Sully's army of over two thousand troops killed over a hundred Santee
and Teton Sioux and burned their village. A rock-mounted plaque tells
the story of the battle.
• **WHITESTONE HILL BATTLEFIELD STATE PARK:** Located east of SH 56
near Merricourt in far southern North Dakota. Sully attacked a village of
some four thousand Yanktonai and Hunkpapa Sioux on September 3,
1863, killing a large number and capturing others before destroying the
village. The battlefield park features the statue of an army bugler blow-
ing taps. An on-site museum contains pictures and relics of the battle.
701–349–3622, 800–222–4766. www.state.nd.us/hist/whitestone

Fort Sites
• **CAMP HANCOCK STATE HISTORIC SITE:** Located at 101 W. Main St.,
Bismarck, established to protect work crews of the Northern Pacific
Railroad. The enlarged and remodeled log headquarters building hous-
es an Interpretive Center. 701–328–9664 or North Dakota Heritage Center,
701–328–2666. www.state.nd.us/hist
• **FORT ABERCROMBIE STATE HISTORIC SITE:** Established by its name-
sake, Lt. Col. John Abercrombie in 1857 in far southeastern North

Dakota, now near the town of Abercrombie off I-29. Having been established to protect the Montana gold field trains, Fort Abercrombie was active at the time of the Minnesota massacre and came under siege by the Sioux for several days during September 1862. One of its original buildings remains, and a blockhouse and palisade fortification have been reconstructed. A museum is located on site. 701–553–8513. www.state.nd.us/hist/abercrombie

• **FORT ABRAHAM LINCOLN:** Located in a state park on the west bank of the Heart River three miles south of Mandan on SH 1806. It was named for the assassinated President. The post's cavalry barracks have been restored, as well as Custer's home while he was commanding officer there. Mandan earth lodges are displayed. State park: 701–667–6340. www.ndparks.com/Parks/FLSP

• **FORT BUFORD STATE HISTORIC SITE:** Located off SH 1804 southwest of present Trenton some two miles from Fort Union. The post's garrison campaigned against the Sioux and Northern Cheyennes, and it was the site of Sitting Bull's surrender in 1881. Today the post features a powder magazine, post cemetery, and two original buildings, one of which contains a museum that features exhibits and video presentations. 701–572–9034. www.state.nd.us/hist/buford

• **FORT CLARK:** Located seven and a half miles southeast of Stanton, the fort was built by the American Fur Company in 1830–1831. The site now contains structure foundations, earth lodge remnants, and a Mandan burial ground. It was named for William Clark, governor of Missouri Territory. 701–794–8832 or North Dakota Heritage Center, 701–328–2666. www.state.nd.us/hist

• **FORT DILTS STATE HISTORIC SITE:** Marker is located west of Rhame in the northwest corner of the state. This former impromptu sod enclosure was constructed when an eighty-wagon party and cavalry escort en route to the Montana gold fields was attacked and held under siege for fourteen days by Sioux Indians in 1864. It is one of the rare forts ever to honor an enlisted soldier by taking the name of Army Scout Cpl. Jefferson Dilts, who died defending his wagon train there.

• **FORT PEMBINA:** This post located near the town of Pembina on the Red River was established in 1870 to monitor the Sioux Indians and halt elicit trade with Canada. It was destroyed by fire in 1895 and abandoned. Fort Pembina Historical Society, PO Box 433, Pembina, ND 58271.

• **FORT RANSOM STATE HISTORIC SITE:** Located in the southeast corner of the state near the town of Fort Ransom and Fort Ransom State Park.

Named for Brig. Gen Thomas Ransom, the post was established in June 1867 to monitor the Sioux and protect Western transportation. Only building locations and a now-dry eight-foot moat remain of the former log and sod stockade. A historical marker is on site. 701–973–4331. www.ndparks.com/Parks/FRSP

• **FORT RICE STATE HISTORIC SITE:** Located on the west bank of the Missouri River off SH 1806 south of the town of Fort Rice, the fort was constructed in 1864 by General Sully during his campaign against the Sioux and dismantled in 1878. It was named for Brig. Gen. James Rice, who was killed in the Civil War. A soldier stationed there wrote: "It is built on a beautiful table of land some 100 feet above the level of the [Missouri] river—a splendid site . . . built of cottonwood logs sawed 6 by 8 (inches) and one story high. There are eight barracks or room for eight companies of soldiers, besides officers' quarters, hospital buildings, etc. The bastions are on the southwest and northeast corners."[1] The post reservation area is now included in a state park. A historical marker is on site.

• **FORT SEWARD STATE HISTORIC SITE:** Established in 1872 on the James River above Jamestown as a supply base for Fort Totten, the facility was abandoned in 1883. It was named for Secretary of State William Seward. The fort served as an Indian school until 1894. The City of Fort Seward sponsors an annual Wagon Train event.

• **FORT TOTTEN STATE HISTORIC SITE:** Located on SH 57 near the town of Fort Totten on the banks of Devils Lake, the post was established in July 1867 to protect transportation to the Montana gold fields and to monitor the reservation Indians. Many of its buildings have been restored, and one now houses an interpretive center. Its namesake was Brig. Gen. Joseph Totten, U.S. Army chief engineer. 701–766–4441. www.state.nd.us/hist/totten

• **FORT UNION TRADING POST NATIONAL HISTORIC SITE:** Fort Union, located southwest from Trenton on SH 1804, was established by the American Fur Company in 1832. The post drew many notable men of the day westward, among them artist George Catlin, and introduced many of the Northern tribes to the ways and effects of the white man. Replicated in total by an Act of Congress, the fort is operated by the National Park Service. It offers a visitor center and the on-site Bourgeois House as well as recreation facilities. 701–572–9083 or 701–572–7622. www.nps.gov/fous

• **FORT YATES:** Located off SH 1806 near the town of Fort Yates on the west bank of the Missouri River in southern North Dakota, the post was established in 1834 to monitor the Standing Rock Indian Agency. It was named for Capt. George W. Yates, Seventh Cavalry, who was killed at the Little Bighorn. The gravesite of Sitting Bull is located near the post site.

Other Sites to See

• **CHASKA STATE HISTORIC SITE:** At this site of Camp Banks three miles north of Driscoll, Chaska, an Indian scout for Gen. Henry W. Sibley, died and was buried in the camp's fortification ditch.

• **DOUBLE DITCH INDIAN VILLAGE STATE HISTORIC SITE:** This site, west of US 83 north of Bismarck near Washburn, displays ancient ruins of a large Mandan earth lodge with refuse mounds and two surrounding fortification ditches still visible. The ruins, such as Lewis and Clark saw, date from the 1675–1780 period. Bismarck, 701–328–2626. www.state.nd.us/hist/doubleditch

• **SACAGAWEA MEMORIAL:** A twelve-foot-high bronze statue of Sacagawea, or Bird Woman, Lewis and Clark's Shoshone guide, stands at the entrance to the North Dakota Heritage Center in Bismarck.

• **SITTING BULL BURIAL STATE HISTORIC SITE:** Site on western edge of Fort Yates marks the original grave (before his remains were reburied south of Mobridge, South Dakota) along with a much-vandalized sculpture of the famous chief.

• **WRITING ROCK:** These two large boulders bearing Indian pictographs are located twelve miles north of Grenora in the northwest corner of the state. They were discovered by Sully's expedition of 1864. Bismarck, 701–224–2666.

Related Museums

• **BISMARCK:** North Dakota Heritage Center, Capitol Grounds, 612 E. Blvd. Ave., Bismarck, N.D. In telling the historical story of North Dakota from the age of dinosaurs to present, the center illuminates Plains Indian life with quill-work collections and other artifacts of a Plains Indian camp. 701–328–3710, or North Dakota Heritage Center 701–328–2666. www.state.nd.us/hist

• **BUFORD:** Missouri-Yellowstone Confluence Interpretive Center, located at Hwys. 58 and 1804, twenty-two miles south of Williston at Fort Buford, features two exhibit galleries, a museum store dedicated to Lewis and Clark, prehistoric life, fur trade era, and Fort Buford with more than two hundred period artifacts. 701–572–9034. www.state.nd.us/hist/lewisclark/attractions_mycic

• **NEW TOWN:** Three Tribes Museum, four miles south of town on the Fort Berthold Indian Reservation in Four Bears Memorial Park, tells the story of the Mandan, Hidatsa, and Arikara tribes who hosted the Lewis and Clark Expedition at the Great Bend of the Missouri River in 1804 and 1806. The tribes raised corn, hunted buffalo, and resided in earthen lodges. 701–627–4477.   http://lewisandclarktrail.com/section2/ndcities/new-town/museum.htm

• **WASHBURN:** Lewis and Clark Interpretive Center, located west of US 83 just north of Washburn and adjacent to the Double Ditch Mandan village ruins. Tours, 701–462–8535 or 877–462–8535. www.fortmandan.com/planningyourvisit/interpretivecenter

Trails to Explore

• **THE MISSOURI RIVER HISTORIC TRAIL:** Though North Dakota's historic sites are spread throughout the state, an interesting tour could extend from the fur trading center of Fort Union and nearby Fort Buford south to the Killdeer Battlefield; then east to the Knife River Indian Village Historic Site, Fort Mandan, and Fort Clark area; then south to Fort Abraham Lincoln State Park; then to the Fort Rice State Historic Site; and on south to the Sitting Bull Burial Site and Fort Yates.

The Fort Yates end of this trail connects to South Dakota historic sites while the Forts Union/Buford end leads to historic trails in Montana.

Still another historic North Dakota trail leads south from Forts Union and Buford at Williston on US 85 to Killdeer and on along the Theodore Roosevelt National Park/Elkhorn Ranch Site to US 12, then west past Rhame and (following road markers) to the Fort Dilts site north of the highway. The Slim Buttes Battle Site off SH 20 can be reached by continuing on into South Dakota and turning east on SH 20.

Note

1. Joseph H. Drips, *Three Years Among the Indians in Dakota* (Kimball, SD: Brule Index, 1894; New York: S. Lewis, 1974), 72–73.

CHAPTER SEVENTEEN

South Dakota
Tour Guide

I n 1817 Joseph LaFramboise established a fur trading post at the mouth of the Teton River, the site of present Pierre, South Dakota. Increased transportation along the river led to conflicts between the fur men and Indians. During 1822, the Arikaras raided a Missouri Fur Company with the loss of two warriors. They were still angry when fur trader William Ashley and his party arrived at their villages the following year. The Arikaras attacked the fur traders and drove them downstream. Ashley suffered fourteen men killed and the loss of much property.

When news of the event reached St. Louis, Col. Henry Leavenworth marched forth with 226 Sixth Infantry troops to punish the Arikaras. A company of fur men and several hundred Sioux warriors, who perpetually warred with the Arikaras, joined Leavenworth's force to form a so-called "Missouri Legion." The Sioux reached the Arikara villages first and attacked them without success. When Leavenworth arrived, he bombarded the village with artillery. A number of Arikaras were killed, and others fled their homes. Though they had long resisted attacks by the Sioux and other tribes, they now retreated northward and established a new village higher up the river.

It could be said that the Indian wars of the West started with the Battle of the Arikara villages and came to a final bloody end in the Dakotas with the Sioux massacre at Wounded Knee.

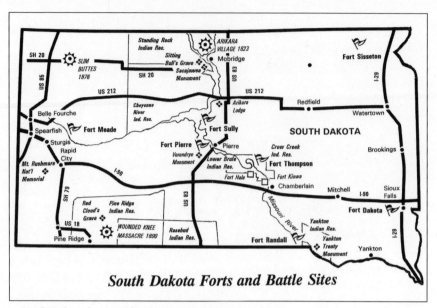

South Dakota forts and battle sites. (Courtesy of author)

Battle Sites

• **ARIKARA VILLAGE:** Monument designating General Leavenworth's attack on the Arikara villages in 1823 was once located on the west bank of the Missouri River some fifteen miles above Mobridge. This was also the site of other conflicts and of the 1825 treaty signing by Gen. Henry Atkinson and Maj. Benjamin O'Fallon. During 2001 the monument was moved to the Klein Museum in Mobridge.

• **SLIM BUTTES:** This site, located in northwestern South Dakota south of the town of Reva on SH 79, retains its natural setting on the edge of the Custer National Forest. State historical markers and a monument commemorate the battle.

• **WOUNDED KNEE:** Located east of the town of Wounded Knee on the Pine Ridge Reservation. This 1890 massacre of a band of Miniconjou Sioux under Chief Big Foot is noted by several plaques and a memorial shaft in the Wounded Knee Cemetery.

Fort Sites

• **FORT DAKOTA:** Established in May 1865 on the west bank of the Big Sioux River near present Sioux Falls, its name was taken from the Dakota

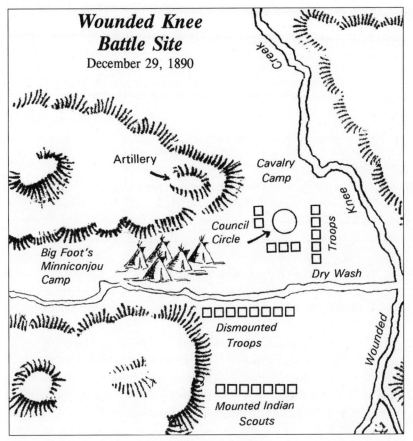

Wounded Knee battle site diagram. (Courtesy of author)

Sioux Indians. A loose collection of log and stone buildings surrounded by a rail fence, it was abandoned in June 1869 and the grounds transferred to the Interior Department. Its historic site is on Phillips Ave., between Seventh and Eighth Streets, in Sioux Falls.

• **FORT HALE:** Located above the town of Fort Lookout on the Missouri River, the fort was founded in 1870 and abandoned in 1884. Originally designated as the Lower Brule Agency, it was renamed for Capt. Owen Hale, Seventh Cavalry, who died in a fight with the Nez Percé in 1877.

• **FORT MEADE:** Located east of Sturgis on SH 34. Established in 1878 to protect white interests in the Black Hills, its Seventh Cavalry garrison played a minor role in the Northern Cheyenne retreat of that year and in 1890 sent troops to Wounded Knee. Named for Maj. Gen. George Meade of Civil War fame, many of its original remnants remain. The Old Fort Meade Historical Association maintains an on-site museum. 605–347–9822 (summer), 605–347–2818 (winter).

• **FORT PIERRE:** Originally constructed in 1831 as a Missouri River trading post and named for Pierre Chouteau Jr., it was purchased and taken over by the U.S. Army in 1855, but because of insufficient forage it was abandoned in 1857. A historical marker is on site.

• **FORT RANDALL:** Located on the Missouri River near the Nebraska border, the fort was established in 1856 to maintain peace among the warring tribes. A monument commemorates a treaty with the Yankton Sioux and others at Fort Randall in 1868. Named for Col. Daniel Randall, army paymaster, its military operation was severely reduced in 1884. Site and marker located on west side of Fort Randall Dam twelve miles west of Wagner on SH 46. Post chapel and cemetery remain with interpretive trail; visitor center provides exhibit of post.

• **FORT SISSETON:** Located at 11545 Northside Drive in the Fort Sisseton State Park northwest of Eden off SH 10, this post was established in 1864 to monitor the Sisseton Indian Reservation and protect frontier settlements and Western transportation. A large number of its original buildings have been restored and refurbished. A visitor center is on site. 605–448–5474 or 605–448–5101. www.sdgfp.info/parks/regions/glaciallakes/fortsisseton

• **FORT SULLY:** The original Fort Sully was constructed by General Sully on the east side of present Pierre across from Farm Island. It was abandoned in 1866, and a new Fort Sully was constructed on the east bank of the Missouri River twenty-eight miles north of Pierre. The new fort, in turn, was abandoned in 1894 and the buildings sold at auction. That site is now flooded. A museum and interpretive center at the original site in the Farm Island State Recreation Area features historical photos and Indian artifacts. 605–224–5605.

• **FORT THOMPSON:** Located on the Crow Creek Indian Reservation, the post was established in 1864 and named for Col. Clark Thompson, Superintendent of Indian Affairs for the region. The post was also known as the Crow Creek Agency. It was abandoned in 1867.

Other Sites of Interest

• **BEAR BUTTE NATIONAL LANDMARK AT STURGIS:** Mountain sacred to many Native Americans, contains recreation trail and visitor center. 605–947–5340 or 605–347–7627. www.state.sd.us/gfp/sdparks/bearbutte

• **CRAZY HORSE MEMORIAL:** The not-yet-finished but monumental sculpture of the famous Lakota leader can be reached on Hwy. 16/385 seventeen miles from Mount Rushmore. Crazy Horse Memorial Foundation: 605–673–4681. www.crazyhorse.org

• **DE SMET:** Laura Ingalls Wilder Memorial, 105 Olivet SE, is dedicated to the memory of the *Little House on the Prairie* series author. 605–854–3383. www.liwms.com

• **RED CLOUD'S GRAVE:** The burial site of this famous Oglala leader is located near the Red Cloud Heritage Center on Cemetery Hill between Oglala and Pine Ridge.

• **SACAGAWEA MONUMENT:** South Dakota's memorial to Sacagawea is located on a bluff across the Missouri River from Mobridge.

• **SITTING BULL'S GRAVE:** Site is marked by seven-ton granite bust of the famous Lakota chief near the South Dakota Sacagawea Monument.

• **JEDEDIAH SMITH MONUMENT:** Monument located at the entrance of Indian Memorial Campground (Smith's Bay) on US 12 west of Mobridge commemorates the great Western trailblazer who discovered and charted the central route from the Rockies to the Pacific Coast.

• **HOT SPRINGS MAMMOTH SITE:** 1800 Hwy. 18 Truck Rt., presents ice age mammoth, camel, and bear remains, plus fossils from a sixty-foot-deep sink hole. 605–745–6017 or 800–325–6991. www.mammothsite.com

• **TRIPLE U RANCH:** Located near Lake Oahe 31 miles northwest of Fort Pierre on SH 1806 at mile marker 217. Site of *Dances with Wolves* filming. The ranch features the largest buffalo herds in the world along with many species of Western wildlife. Buffalo hunts are held in the fall. 605–567–3624. www.tripleuranch.com

Related Museums

• **ABERDEEN:** Dacotah Prairie Museum, 213 S. Main St., presents Native American and local history materials. 605–626–7117.

• **BROOKINGS:** South Dakota Art Museum, at Medary Ave. and Harvey Dunn St., offers collections of Native American art and displays. 605–688–5423. www3.sdstate.edu/Administration/SouthDakotaArtMuseum

• **CHAMBERLAIN:** The Akta Lakota Museum, Exit 263 off I-90, presents various aspects of Lakota culture. 605–734–3455 or 800–778–3452. www.aktalakota.org

• **CUSTER:** Four Mile Old West Town, Rt. 1, provides military and Buffalo Soldier history, photos, stockade. 605–673–3905. www.four-milesd.com/history

• **GETTYSBURG:** Dakota Sunset Museum, 2050 W. Commercial, offers historical artifacts, including the Sioux Medicine Rock. 605–765–9480. www.sdhistory.org/soc/Hist_Orgs/gettysburg

• **MOBRIDGE:** Klein Museum, 1820 W. Grand Crossing (US 12 west of town), specializes in Native American and pioneer history. Features account of Teton Sioux under Fool Soldier who rescued a group of white captives from the Santee Sioux Indians and returned them to their families. 605–845–7243.

• **PIERRE:** Cultural Heritage Center of South Dakota, 900 Governor's Drive, offers written records and artifacts of American Indian heritage with exhibits such as the Oyate Tawicho'an (Ways of the People) exhibit and replica of the Jefferson Peace Medals presented to the tribes by Lewis and Clark. 605–773–3458. www.state.sd.us/state/capitol/cultural

• **PINE RIDGE INDIAN RESERVATION:** Red Cloud Indian School Heritage Center, campus of Holy Rosary Mission/Red Cloud Indian School, four and a half miles north of Pine Ridge, displays paintings, graphics, sculptures, and bead and porcupine quill work of Indian artists along with Oglala Sioux legends and history. The grave of Oglala chief Red Cloud overlooks the school from a nearby hilltop. 605–867–5491. www.redcloud-school.org/museum

• **RAPID CITY:** Journey Museum, 222 New York St., Sioux Indian Museum operated under the Board of Arts and Crafts of the U.S. Department of Interior and featuring the work of contemporary Sioux artists. 605–394–6923. www.journeymuseum.org

• **SPEARFISH:** High Plains Western Heritage Center, Exit 14 S., I-90. Five-state (South Dakota, North Dakota, Nebraska, Wyoming, Montana) regional museum features Western artifacts from the Plains Indian period through the discovery of gold and the open-range cattle industry. 605–642–9378. www.westernheritagecenter.com

• **TIMBER LAKE:** Museum holds collections of Indian artifacts, photos, wood carvings, and bronzes. 605–865–3246.

• **YANKTON:** Lewis and Clark Visitor Center, located on Nebraska side of Gavins Point Dam, tells story of fur trade, tribes living along the river, and journey of Lewis and Clark. 402–667–7873, ext. 3246. http://lewisand-clarktrail.com/section2/sdcities/Yankton/LCVisitor

Trails to Explore

• **THE WOUNDED KNEE TRAIL:** Taking the Wounded Knee Battle Site north of US 18 east of Pine Ridge as a primary point of interest in the

Plains Indian Wars of South Dakota, a tourist can travel from there north on US 385 and US 85 (Mount Rushmore, the Crazy Horse Memorial, the Black Hills National Caves, and Fort Meade offer potential side trips en route) to Spearfish, then take Scenic Trail I-90 to SH 20 and east through the Custer National Forest to the Slim Buttes Battle Site (located south of SH 20, west of SH 70 intersection).

Driving east from the Slim Buttes sites will lead through the Cheyenne River Sioux Indian Reservation and the Standing Rock Indian Reservation to Mobridge, which features the sites of Sitting Bull's Grave, Sacagawea Monument, and the Leavenworth Monument. En route, a short side trip west on US 212 offers the replica of an Arikara lodge at West Whitlock Recreation Area.

From Mobridge, US 12 (east) and US 83 (south) lead to Pierre, where the Verendyre Monument, the Klein Museum, and the unrestored site of Fort Pierre are featured. Farther southwest are the Lower Brule Indian Reservation and below them the undeveloped Lewis and Clark sites of Forts Defiance, Hale, and Kiowa. The unrestored site of Fort Thompson is located at the town of Fort Thompson on the Crow Creek Indian Reservation. Picturesque buffalo herds graze at the Triple U Ranch and on the two Indian reservations. A tour brochure for the area can be obtained at the Chamberlain Information Center on I-90 or at the Chamber of Commerce, 115 W. Lawler Ave.

INDEX